RETHINKING
THE
CORPORATION

RETHINKING THE CORPORATION

THE ARCHITECTURE OF CHANGE

ROBERT M. TOMASKO

amacom

American Management Association

New York • Atlanta • Boston • Chicago • Kansas City • San Francisco • Washington, D.C.
Brussels • Toronto • Mexico City

This publication is designed to provide accurate and authoritative information in regard to the subject matter covered. It is sold with the
understanding that the publisher is not engaged in rendering legal,
accounting, or other professional service. If legal advice or other expert
assistance is required, the services of a competent professional person
should be sought.

Library of Congress Cataloging-in-Publication Data

Tomasko, Robert M.
   Rethinking the corporation : the architecture of change / Robert
M. Tomasko.
       p.   cm.
   Includes bibliographical references and index.
   ISBN 0-8144-5022-9
   1. Organizational change.   2. Corporate reorganizations.
I. Title.
HD58.8.T65   1993
658.4'063—dc20   93-9246
                                                          CIP

Printing number

10   9   8   7   6   5   4   3   2   1

Contents

Acknowledgments

"What do you plan to write about after producing a book called *Downsizing?*" This is a question many of my clients and colleagues have asked. None felt the global economy was ready for something about "upsizing," and few thought that streamlining alone was sufficient to produce an organization strong enough to survive until the start of the new century.

These conversations started me on a four-year journey, visiting several dozen companies that had undertaken major organizational restructurings and had come out of them stronger and more competitive. The objective was to learn about not only especially effective structures and management practices but the change process itself—which steps seemed most important, which were blind alleys, and which were prerequisites for the others.

The search was worldwide. It began in the outskirts of Paris at Carrefour, the amazingly successful French company that created the "hypermarket" retail concept—along with an exemplary approach to decentralization that allowed it to thrive worldwide—and it ended in Tokyo, where I had a chance to examine the ambitious plans of a Japanese manufacturer to dramatically reshape its headquarters and its research functions.

Between these end points in my investigation, many senior executives took time from their crowded schedules to talk about how they managed organizational change and to react to some of my early ideas. To encourage candor—I was equally interested in what did not work and what did—I promised to keep these interviews confidential. However, there are several executives to whom it is appropriate to express my gratitude publicly: Cesar Bonamico (Brastemp), Jean-Luc Chereau (Carrefour), Angel Casan Marcos (Grupo Industrial Alfa), Gary Donahee (Northern Telecom), Ken Faber (Ford), Bob Franklin (Ontario Hydro), Marvin Goodman (Liptons International), Jacques Goyer (Office of the Auditor General of Canada), Floris Maljers (Unilever), Dean Minter (Illinois Bell), Stephen Perry (Food Marketing Institute), Raymond Smith (Bell Atlantic), George Sherman (formerly of Black & Decker), Bill Stiritz

(Ralston Purina), Sir John Sainsbury (Sainsbury's), Carlos Salvatori (Citicorp), Nigel Travis (Grand Metropolitan), and Stefan Winsnes (Scandinavian Airlines).

My interests in organization design, career structures, and the virtues of hierarchy were sparked in graduate school seminars given by Paul Lawrence, Harry Levinson, Edgar Schein, and Abraham Zaleznik. For these people's help in focusing my attention on the organization issues that really matter, I am most grateful. Herman Stein's generous invitation to assist him while he was a fellow at the Center for Advanced Study in the Behavioral Sciences many years ago started what has become a long-term interest in the role of professionals in organizations. Some of the seeds he planted in our conversations at the Center have ripened into many of the ideas I present in Chapter 10 about ways to have influence without being a manager.

This book draws parallels between the approaches of the architect and those of the organization designer. I am not an architect, but I have found it very useful to examine my work as a management consultant through the lens of another profession. This interest also began in graduate school, where I had an opportunity to study with Martin Rein and Donald Schön how architects learn to do architecture. I have also had several opportunities to be on the receiving end of both the services and the friendship of architects. I am grateful for these busy professionals' willingness to put up with more questions than were absolutely necessary to get their jobs done or to keep our conversations moving. Special thanks go to Philip Escoff, Joseph Migiani, Joan Riordan, Lew Schwartz, Robert Schwartz, and Ken Walker.

My affiliation for more than a decade with Arthur D. Little, Inc., has provided many opportunities to discover and test out a number of the ideas presented here. I am grateful for the support of Charles Lamantia, Arthur D. Little's chief executive, who showed me that it is possible for a consultant to practice what he preaches. The longtime friendship and encouragement of Jean-Philippe Deschamps, Ranganath Nayak, and Harland Riker were also key to my being able to complete this project.

I have been especially fortunate that a number of my colleagues in Arthur D. Little's offices worldwide made it possible for me to meet with their clients and with the leaders of many major corporations around the globe. In the guise of sharing over dinner ideas from my earlier book on downsizing, I was also able to elicit some of these executives' best thinking about the directions businesses need to take after completing a restructuring. These sessions were held in Amsterdam, Brussels, Copenhagen, The Hague, London, Mexico City, Monterrey, São Paulo, Singapore, Tokyo, Wiesbaden, and Zurich.

For their help in arranging these meetings I want to thank: Roberto Batres, Mike Carman, Moyses Gedanke, Maurice Olivier, Dermot McMeekin, Tom Sommerlatte, Nick Steinthal, Michael Younger, Martin van der Mandele, Roger Wippermann, and Yoshimichi Yamashita.

A similar opportunity was provided by Right Associates, one of the largest providers of outplacement assistance, which arranged a series of idea exchange sessions with human resources executives in thirty-one cities throughout the United States and Canada. For these my appreciation goes to: Geoff Boole, Joe Bowden, Larry Evans, Rob Fish, Nancy Geffner, Peter Hainline, Virginia Lord, Frank Louchheim, Warren Radtke, Tom Shea, Terry Szwec, François Van Vyve, and George Whitwell.

I have had a lot of help preparing this book from Adrienne Hickey, my editor at AMACOM, as well as from my family. Adrienne skillfully assisted in countless ways to shape a big subject into a book-sized format. She must have been in close communication with my wife, Brenda Turnbull, because at home Brenda's comments about chapter length and organization mirrored hers. Brenda also taught me that the most useful way to get one book actually written, after accumulating several years of research notes, was to put aside for later all the otherwise interesting material that really belongs in another book.

Our children had a part to play also. Laura freely shared the techniques she learned in first and second grade of "mind-mapping" and "conferencing." They are great ways to overcome temporary writer's block. Her younger sister, Julia, took a different tack. Whenever she would see me leafing through a magazine or otherwise avoiding writing, she would gently, but firmly, say: "Get to work on that book, mister." William, our two-year-old, has only one job in the house: to look cute. This he accomplished extraordinarily well, always reminding me there was a lot of fun awaiting this book's completion.

The real cost of writing is measured in missed family dinners and soccer and Little League games, as well as in vacations on which Dad finds it necessary to pack a portable computer and in opportunities to visit his mother that become near-impossible to schedule. These are costs borne much more by the author's family than by the writer. For my family's willingness to incur these, and for doing it with grace and understanding, I am appreciative beyond words. To them, this book is dedicated.

For centuries, large organizations have modeled themselves after the pyramid—the structure used by the ancient Egyptians to entomb their dead leaders.

Photo courtesy of the Egyptian Tourist Authority.

Prologue

Lower Walls

*Minimize the internal and external boundaries
that stand in the way of work getting done.*

Getting the organization right is a concern held by many in this era of global restructuring. This is a very difficult time to work in, or to manage, a corporation. Downsizings and restructurings have become widespread, but their purpose has usually been short-term chipping away at old structures and practices. Too few have been guided by a clear vision of what kind of new corporation needs to emerge from this turmoil and chaos.

This is also a time in which quick-fix solutions, gimmicks, and loosely thought-out recommendations abound.

This book does not attempt to add to these. Instead, it suggests a process corporations and their managers can use to move the organization from where it is now to where they feel it needs to be. It looks cautiously at ideas about flat structures, empowerment, reengineering, and teamwork; highlights their prerequisites; and distinguishes nice-sounding slogans from workable practices.

It provides a blueprint for organization planners—but one that highlights the steps of the planning process, instead of presenting a plan into which every business is expected to be force-fitted.

It argues for a rethinking—from the top down and the bottom up— of the assumptions that determine how many corporations are organized and managed.

This rethinking is not just an academic exercise. Corporations are the institutions that the public in much of the world has entrusted to champion its economic security. But in too many cases nineteenth-century structures are being expected to cope with twenty-first-century challenges. Many of us work in the information age, but the jobs we occupy have not been rethought since the Industrial Revolution.

This book is written for two audiences: those with the power to bring about change in their organizations and those on the receiving end of these changes. As many companies practice decentralization and empowerment, the number of people in the first of these groups is dramatically increasing. Concern with getting the organization right is no longer limited to the chief executive and a small circle of advisors. They may set an overall direction and shape the broad outline of the superstructure, but then the job of organization planner cascades down the ranks. Even individual contributors are increasingly being asked to structure their own jobs—and to keep adapting the structure to fit changes in business needs.

For readers with more limited ways of influencing their company's direction and their job's design, this book is a guide to what changes are occurring and why. It also offers a preview of what influences may significantly shape their own jobs and careers in the future.

The book encourages the reader to look at the task of organizational overhaul the way an architect might approach the design of a building. Architects are very skilled at managing the design process, in coping with multiple constraints, and in using know-how from many disciplines to shape structures that work.

Shaping the New Corporation

What will be the shape of the new corporation—the company that survives and thrives on the difficult path to the twenty-first century? Will it be a flattened pyramid, a networked cluster, a hollowed-out donut, or possibly even a shamrock?

These and other nonhierarchical possibilities stiumlate a great deal of interesting speculation. The art of organization design is at a significant crossroads. Many of its old truisms are coming under fire, and few new proven ones have emerged to replace them. But at least some sense of direction for the new corporation is apparent: *It will be a business with few walls*. Its structure will minimize barriers between staff thinkers and line doers, between functions and divisions, and between the company and the outside world.

The Old Breed of Corporation

Many assumptions that have served as basic building blocks for the corporation in the one-strategy-at-a-time, mass-production era are either inadequate or misleading in an era of surprise-based competition. This conventional wisdom, which has become too dangerous to take for granted, includes a variety of beliefs that have shaped the organization structures of the twentieth century. How many of these have currency in your company?

- Bigger is better: The size and scope of the company are limited only by the imagination of its leaders or by the forbearance of its lenders.
- The best way to get something done is in-house, using an organization built around functionally discrete activities.
- The basic building block of organization is the individual job.
- Standards can be maintained only by keeping employees in narrowly defined and closely watched jobs.
- The key functions of the middle manager are control and coordination.
- The kind of information that you should have is determined by your place in the management hierarchy.
- Career advancement means moving upward in this management hierarchy. If you want to influence the direction of the business, become a manager.

These and similar assumptions implicitly guide the ways most companies are organized today. They all encourage *corporate wall building*. Some of these assumptions build barriers between different classes of workers. Others separate the broad range of skills many employees bring to their work from the narrow demands of their jobs. Some lay out well-demarcated internal turf boundaries, others keep the business divided from potential external resources and allies. And some operate more on a psychological level, keeping valid information and learning away from those who need it most. What kind of companies have we built by applying these assumptions?

Steven Hronec, of the accounting firm Arthur Andersen & Company, has observed that many companies "design a product by throwing it over the wall from one department to another." Each toss adds costs and delays as well as distance between the final product and the original requirements of the customer. The characteristics of this process are replicated in the way most businesses handle new orders, develop annual budgets, orient promising new hires, and put together finished products.

The structure of many jobs, departments, and functions frequently offers only impediments to the flow of work, the generation of new ideas, and the growth of commitment to the overall mission of the business. But we still tend to use old definitions and structures as our basic units of organization. This is partially a result of mental inertia on the part of organization planners, but it also occurs because these structures offer some sense of comfort, security, and control.

Corporate Maginot Lines — The Fortress Mentality

André Maginot was a French civil servant. He also served as a soldier during the horribly bloody battle at Verdun during World War I. He and thousands of others held back the repeated German attacks on Verdun's massive fortifications, but not without being seriously wounded. Maginot recovered, continued his government career, and in 1929 became France's minister of war. Then, for the next few years, he directed the construction of a long line of thick concrete forts and underground bunkers that paralleled France's border with Germany. Maginot credited the walls of Verdun with saving his life and expected what came to be known as the Maginot Line to do the same for France.

When the Germans attacked France again in 1940, Maginot's wall proved irrelevant. The Germans simply went around it, attacked through Belgium, and overran French defenses in a matter of weeks.

Much of history is the story of the erection of walls, the creation of a temporary sense of security and control, and the eventual collapse of the barricades. The famous walled city of Jericho succumbed to a combination of trumpets and psychological warfare; China's Great Wall was penetrated by Genghis Khan; many medieval castles met their match when cannons were invented. Still, given these failings, the value of temporary security is high, for walls continue to be popular to propose and build. The debate around the "Star Wars" plan to put a wall of satellites in space illustrates this well.

Just as the business world has adopted the idea of hierarchy from the military, it has reflected in many of its organizations the fortress mentality of armies that are ultimately destined to be outflanked. These corporate Maginot Lines may provide needed order in the short run but can put at risk the business's long-term health.

John Welch, General Electric's chief executive, likes to characterize organizational walls as "tollgates." He goes to great lengths in his speeches to General Electric's managers to emphasize the high cost of the walls' tariffs. He feels that whenever people or products are forced to cross a wall, they pay a toll, in economic, emotional, or time costs. These costs eventually lead to higher prices and diminished competitiveness.

What is the opposite of this situation? What is a company with minimal walls? It is an enterprise that has oriented itself to prize *speed, flexibility,* and *focus.*

It has done this by eliminating the costly barriers that have isolated it from its customers, suppliers, and marketplace partners. It has also eliminated the internal obstacles that have separated its employees, managers, and organization units from each other.

It is one that has rethought both processes and practices. The leader of the IDS subsidiary of American Express, Harvey Golub, envisions a situation where "there's something about the culture—not just the knowledge but the way it gets applied—that gives the organization skills beyond the talent of the people."

Making the whole more than the sum of its parts is a hope of many corporate executives. But getting there can prove difficult.

Attempts to Leap the Walls—Finding Models for the Future

The mindless following of barrier-building assumptions has been a source of trouble for many companies. Another is the simplistic seductiveness of many contemporary ideas about the company of the future. Many of these ideas rightly take aim directly at the evils of bureaucratic walls. But then they became the management gurus' equivalent of the storming of the Bastille: When the prison's walls were surmounted, few prisoners were actually found inside needing to be released.

Some business best-sellers advocate equally romantic and symbolic ideas about the company of the future. Chaos, and how organizations must join forces with it to survive, is one such popular topic. Some books suggest the path to success is in some way related to the process by which large creatures learn how to dance. Some put conflict on a pedestal and suggest the cultivation and harnessing of tension as the answer. Others point toward the symphony orchestra as the corporate model of the future. Many see teams—and clusters of teams— as the only sound way to organize work.

One pair of forward-thinking management writers, Stan Davis and Bill Davidson—possibly perplexed by all these alternatives—feel the best thing to do now with many dysfunctional organizations is nothing. Let them collapse of their own excess weight. The writers lament the state of modern organization theory: "The old models don't work, and the new ones have yet to evolve."

It has become politically correct among many business thinkers to reject hierarchy and to lionize the flat organization. But seldom is attention given to discerning when and how much hierarchy might be appropriate. Few guidelines exist for defining how work is to be done, performance to be measured, and careers to flow in these minimalist structures. And almost never are ideas fleshed out about how to get from today's bureaucracy to tomorrow's hot-wired, information-based organization.

There are many stimulating, positive attributes associated with this kind of futuristic thinking. Practicality, however, is not always among them.

Many of these visions fail to appreciate the hard reality of dynamic conservatism, a phenomenon labeled in the 1960s by Donald Schön, a professor at the Massachusetts Institute of Technology and an ex-Arthur D. Little consultant, when he investigated why it is so hard for good ideas to gain acceptance in large organizations. His studies looked at corporations, the military, and civilian bureaucracies. He found that the problem was not usually inertia, the tendency of objects to keep moving in their present course, but a stronger and more pervasive force, a tendency to fight vigorously to remain stable.

A danger lies in too quickly writing off this phenomenon as simple resistance to change, which can be overcome by ignoring it and plowing straight ahead, by trying to pacify it with several well-delivered motivatinal speeches, or by a quick series of team-building meetings. Mastering change requires more than exhortations about initiative, entrepreneurship, and empowerment.

All established social systems—a category that includes successful corporations—work very hard to survive. They, often at great cost, maintain their boundaries, work methods, and patterns of interactions. The more they are pressed from the outside, the more they tend to push back. The need for social equilibrium is very strong, regardless of some commentators' attempts to deny it, and is frequently self-reinforcing. This parallels the common biological perspective on what keeps organisms cohesive: *Any tendency toward change is automatically met by increased effectiveness of the factors that resist change.*

Why is this tendency so often ignored when people think about organization change? One reason is the limited understanding of social and psychological dynamics possessed by many would-be "change agents." Psychological intelligence is seldom given the attention in business schools that financial manipulation receives. Furthermore, businesspeople tend to be an optimistic lot. Those who have reached positions of power usually have had more successes than failures in their careers and feel reasonable in extrapolating from their own experiences to situations occurring around them.

What they may not realize is that these experiences, and the often single-minded focus that accompanied them, are less common than they think. Most mere mortals are better jugglers of multiple priorities than single-objective sprinters. Career, family, personal life, professional calling—all tend to blur the agendas of most organization members. And the situation is compounded by the competing priorities of departments, divisions, and other subgroups within the company. Sometimes it takes most of the energy available to just stay on an even keel. Just ask any member of a two-career household.

But what if, instead of rejecting an organization's, and its employees', need for at least a measure of stability, we try to acknowledge, accept, and take advantage of this need? The best defense against a pervasive problem is an equally pervasive understanding of it. What approach can best build this understanding into the new corporation?

We began by considering what is an appropriate shape for the new corporation. Perhaps this is the wrong question, especially since it seems so difficult to settle on a single, always appropriate answer. No one organization design is right for every business; there is too much variation in missions, strategies, and capabilities. The real issue is not so much specifying a new, innovative configuration each company must adopt but outlining a path *each business can follow to invent its unique and best organizational form.* The exact shape may be less important than the process used to discover it.

A Threefold Strategy—A Three-Part Book

If an architect were faced with the problem of revitalizing an aging, dysfunctional corporate structure and were told that the result had to minimize barriers and walls, what steps would be taken? Figure 1 suggests a possible answer.

Applying design logic to reorganization suggests, first, careful consideration of what is already in place, how functional it is, and what turf it needs to cover. The key issue here is *resizing*, adjusting the company's equivalent of the architect's "site" to fit the demands of its future mission. This is the subject of Part One of this book.

Then comes the work of *reshaping*, designing the basic building blocks of the company and arranging them to have the most favorable impact on competitive advantage. This is where traditional corporate reorganization usually begins and ends: rearranging the lines and boxes on the chart. This middle step is necessary, but not sufficient, to remake a corporation. Doing it successfully is still important and requires taking a hard look at the way many companies have overlearned the lessons of the Industrial Revolution. Reshaping is the subject of Part Two.

Figure 1. Similarities between the work of architects and that of organization planners.

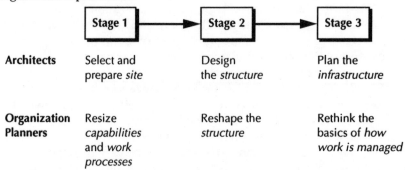

	Stage 1	Stage 2	Stage 3
Architects	Select and prepare *site*	Design the *structure*	Plan the *infrastructure*
Organization Planners	Resize *capabilities* and *work processes*	Reshape the structure	Rethink the basics of *how work is managed*

Finally comes *rethinking* the basics of how the work of the corporation needs to be managed. Just as the architect considers the infrastructure of the building being designed, the organization planner's job is not finished until fresh thought is given to issues such as how concern for the business's future can be mapped onto the organization; how the contributions of nonmanagement "knowledge workers" will be accommodated in the company's power structure, and how authority, careers, and information will flow. These form the infrastructure of the modern corporation and are as critical to its functioning as are the climate control, electrical, lighting, plumbing, and communications systems incorporated into a building's construction plan. Part Three of this book deals with what needs to change in a corporation's infrastructure to guarantee the success of its resizing and reshaping.

These three steps need to occur in an orderly sequence. Modifying the shape of the company's structure makes sense only after the resizing of the work is tackled. As Peter Drucker is fond of saying: "It is always amazing how many of the things we do will never be missed. . . . And nothing is less productive than to make more efficient what should not be done at all."

Just as it is important to lay the groundwork for reorganization, it is equally essential to follow up changes in organization structure with improvements in the basic processes used to manage. Unless these infrastructural aspects of the company are reexamined—and in some cases reinvented—it is very likely the results of restructuring will unravel.

Chapter 1

Create a New Breed
of Corporation

Use the logic of the architect to build speed, flexibility, and focus into the organization structure.

The problem of reshaping a corporation is essentially a problem of design.

In a number of ways the field of architecture provides a good source of perspective on the task of reorganization. The architect provides a master plan for each project and then coordinates the work of many skilled trades and disciplines. While there is room in the design process for art and creativity, few architects have the freedom to start with a clean slate and impose their design on the environment. The architect of a building is usually more driven by the wishes of the client, the purpose of the building, the needs of its inhabitants, the constraints of the site, and the concerns of the regulators. Good architecture is essentially a highly skilled balancing act. On a day-to-day basis, architects match a concern for beauty with a need for energy conservation, the multiplicity of owner-specified requirements with the budget available.

In their actual planning and design work, architects also balance competing structural forces. Buildings must bear a variety of loads and use structure to redistribute them. They must support themselves (their "dead weight"), deal with the comings and goings of their inhabitants ("live weight"), and be prepared to resist sudden pressures from windstorms and earthquakes ("dynamic weight"). They must also cope with more hidden, slow-acting challenges, such as thermal expansion and settling ground. (See Figure 2 for an illustration of these forces.) And what other profession has had more experience in safely removing walls?

Figure 2. The competing loads that structures must bear.

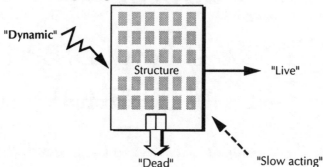

Practicing Organizational Architecture

Certainly, I am not suggesting that the job of corporate reorganization be contracted out to a nearby architect. Architects are, obviously, better trained at manipulating the physical environment than the human one. But there is something to be gained by letting the design mentality of the architect guide, at least metaphorically, the work of the executive or manager as he or she reshapes the corporation.

Organizational architects may work with different materials than do planners of buildings and bridges, but they still are in the business of design. They also balance competing requirements and must marry the company's mission with the principles of human behavior. They must plan structures that can distribute a variety of "loads": employee needs, executives' wishes, market demands, competitor attacks. They must minimize dead weight (bureaucracy and internally directed activities) and maximize the corporation's ability to handle live loads: customer requests and resources needed to meet them. Organizational architects must create companies that can withstand dynamic factors, such as fast and aggressive competitors, while remaining alert to slower-moving dangers, such as technological advances and global economic shifts.

Architects frequently deal with redesign or renovation, not just new construction. This is often true in times of a weak economy. Organization architects, especially during business downturns, often face the task of reorganization. Few have the luxury of creating a business from scratch. Architects are realists. They want to see things happen; they cannot afford to write off an unimplemented good idea as the victim of "resistance to change." For them, inertia and stability-seeking tendencies are *tools to work with,* not just *barriers to overcome.*

Analog Devices' Chairman Ray Stata sees the role of senior executives as increasingly including the planning of their organization:

> Historically leaders were referred to as "captains of the ship" to denote their role in operating the vessel entrusted to their care. But future leaders must be both designers and operators. Their principal contribution will be to shape the design of the organization structure. . . . Expertise in organization design will be a critical skill—a skill that will require considerable technical knowledge about how to analyze, modify, and stimulate the behavior of complex human systems.

This critical skill is not one that is applied once and then forgotten. Organization planning is an ongoing management activity—and not just by senior executives. It requires the same attention given to other strategically significant processes in the corporation, such as new product development, long-range planning, and quality management. It can benefit from attention to continuous improvement, just as products and manufacturing processes do. And it can be guided by lessons drawn from the history and the methods of the building architect.

The Architecture of Change and the Architecture of Stability

When applying the design process to organization planning it is helpful to think about a company having two "architectures," each needing to coexist with the other.

One is an architecture of stability. Organizationally it has been represented by tall, pyramidal hierarchies and narrowly defined jobs. Its role had been to cope with the "dead" and "live" loads imposed on the business. When stronger forces affect the business ("dynamic" or "slow-acting" forces such as deregulation or globalization), stability becomes more of a vice than a virtue, and the second architecture—an architecture of change—needs to come into play.

Too often movement from one to the other has been triggered by a jarring crisis, not a smoothly managed process of adaptation. Few companies are organized well enough to systematically abandon old ways of operating and embrace the necessary new ones. Most companies deal with change by abruptly moving from one architecture of stability to another.

Sometimes this is effective, especially when the major change is anticipated and planned far in advance. This is similar to the approach taken in Japan to keep the temple at Ise in good condition. Originally built in the eighth century A.D., throughout most of its history the temple has been completely dismantled every twenty years, then rebuilt from new materials on an adjoining site. The current shrine is a faithful replica of the original one, without the wear and tear of over a thousand years of use. The regularity of its rebuilding also represents a view of time and change that says these are not enemies to be resisted, but realities to be accepted and adapted to.

An appreciation of the architecture of change is also evident in many Western buildings. A visit to the headquarters of the Internationale Nederlanden Bank (the ING building) alone is almost worth the trip to Amsterdam. Rather than constructing a monolithic forty-three-floor pyramidal office tower, this bank chose to create a more horizontally oriented structure of ten towers of varying heights, all linked to form an "s" shape that winds its way through a neighborhood of shops and houses. The plastic, almost sculptural impression the building gives to passersby—hardly any wall in the building is vertical—mirrors the flexible uses made of the interior work space by the bank's staff of 2,500.

The recent placement of I. M. Pei's modernistic glass pyramid in the courtyard of the centuries-old Louvre in Paris is another example of adaptive architecture (see Figure 3), as is the conversion of the Orsay railroad station across the Seine from the Louvre into a dramatic space to display Impressionist art. In the United States, where monumental railroad stations outnumber the trains running through them, several structures have been recycled very effectively into shopping and hotel complexes.

Building this fluidity and flexibility into organizational structures is often more difficult. But not impossible. It does require a systematic rethinking of most organizational structures so that they explicitly recognize the importance of time as well as turf. Good architecture, whether for buildings or organizations, requires a blend of short-term stability with long-term adaptation.

The Architectural Versus the Engineering Perspective

The Prologue noted that many current ideas about the organization of the future are simplistic and often impractical. But some of the new thinking about organization is, to give it its fair due, a reasonable reaction to the problems inherent in the old, mechanistic models of organization. These models, as London Business School professor Charles Handy maintains, perceive organizations as "gigantic pieces of engi-

Figure 3. I. M. Pei's modern glass pyramid amid the courtyard of the Louvre.

neering, with largely interchangeable human parts." This static view is pervasive among many executives and the management consultants they have used to advise them on matters of organization. "Let's redraw the chart and get back to business as usual" is the approach frequently taken to reorganization. The career paths of many individuals from both consulting and management have passed through engineering schools. Even Tom Peters, whose views are far from those of traditional consultants, holds a bachelor's and a master's degree in engineering.

Many well-intentioned critiques of today's companies come from individuals with behavioral science inclinations: psychologists, anthropologists, and practitioners in the hybrid field of organizational behavior. They have added important missing pieces to our understanding of corporate organization, but their diagnoses tend to be stronger than their prescriptions.

Since the 1980s, individuals with a grounding in information systems and computer networking have given attention to the problems of malfunctioning corporations. Some are advocates of "reengineering," another very useful but narrow and potentially static path to organization improvement. Their tools are powerful but sometimes give too much attention to new technology at the expense of the human change that needs to accompany its introduction.

This situation is a bit like the story of the group of blind men, each touching a different part of an elephant and each providing a different, though myopically accurate, description of the beast.

To generate new thinking about the new corporation, a mind-set is required that blends these alternative perspectives and uses them to shape, or reshape, the business. The issue is not one of simply moving from one narrow perspective—mechanistic engineering—to another— humanistic psychology. Rather, a discipline oriented to melding the work of many fields to create something new is required. Consider the ways architects have evolved new structural forms as new building materials have become available.

The Shape of a Structure Depends on What It's Made From

Structural forms and building materials are *mutually interdependent*. A change of material frequently necessitates a change in structural design. Ancient Egyptian buildings were much larger than those constructed by the ancient Greeks. The Egyptians used granite, plentiful in the cliffs near the Nile River, while the Greeks were limited to the weaker marble, which could not support openings as wide as those the Egyptians favored and which required a different design. Later the Romans, possibly attempting to outdo both predecessor civilizations, perfected the vaulted arch, which allowed for even more massive construction projects than those developed by the Egyptians. The arch could also be built from readily available river basin clay, which allowed the Romans to use this structural form throughout the lands they conquered in Europe and the Middle East.

As Christianity spread, this barrel-like style of building, called Romanesque, became the accepted mode for cathedral design. It worked well in southern Europe, where the sunlight was bright enough to penetrate the tiny window openings permitted by this massive structural style. But in northern Europe, shorter summers and bleaker weather made Romanesque-style buildings fairly dark places. Big windows were indicated, but cutting them into a vault-shaped building led to dangerous structural weaknesses.

In the twelfth century, a new structure was invented to circumvent these difficulties. What eventually came to be called Gothic architecture made use of an innovative structural device, the flying buttress, that provided support for the weight of the cathedral's roof. It even allowed for lesser quantities of expensive stone to be used during the building process without affecting structural integrity. Cathedrals built using flying buttresses (Figure 4) looked as though their skeletons were hung outside their bodies, but the awkwardness of this shape was more than compensated for by the high walls of stained glass now possible because the church's walls no longer bore the roof load. The spacious high ceilings and shafts of multicolored light from the large windows changed the experience of worship for many in the Middle Ages.

As beautiful as the cathedrals at Chartres, France, and Cologne, Germany, are inside, they are massive on the outside. A more streamlined exterior had to await the development in the nineteenth century of new structural materials: mass-produced iron and steel. These materials made possible buildings full of light, such as London's Crystal Palace, and structures designed for height without bulk, like the Eiffel Tower in Paris.

Just as architectural design has developed through this interplay of structure and material, organization design has evolved from simple,

Figure 4. A flying buttress.

family-based forms through functional and divisional configurations to global matrices and other hybrids—each emerging, as did architectural styles, to solve a problem created by its predecessor. New, creative structures, both organizational and architectural, have had to await the development of new building materials, or new ways to think about work, teams, and managers. They have also needed the stimulation of challenging new objectives, just as the vision of a church full of light held by Abbot Sugar in twelfth-century France drove his invention of the flying buttress. Contemporary organization builders are equally stimulated by concerns about speed, flexibility, and focus. Many have begun to refashion the building blocks of their corporations, but progress in inventing new ways to configure these raw materials has lagged.

The Uses of Structure

One reason for the delay in devising new ways to structure companies is the common belief that organization structure is unimportant or something to be viewed as the devil's creation, worthy only of complete elimination. The word "bureaucracy" is a dirty word, even among some bureaucrats. Tom Peters and a number of other popular management gurus have contributed to this bias. Peters directly brands structure as a deadly force, warning that "structure kills."

Peters is certainly on the mark when he discusses activities that are inappropriately structured or hierarchies that are excessively layered. But the baby is in danger of being lost with the bathwater if these instances of structural misuse lead to the assumption that getting the structure right is a concern that can be simply waved aside. Flexibility and adaptability are key attributes of the new corporation, but a totally formless or free-form organization is not necessarily the best way of achieving them. Economic success is usually driven by balancing focus and flexibility. Focus results from decisions about what capabilities need to be marshaled to serve what markets and the extent to which these decisions are reflected in how power is distributed in the company.

Structure, among other things, serves to designate turf lines, accountability boundaries. It provides channels for directing the use of a business's capabilities. This is something many savvy operating executives instinctively appreciate and use effectively as a management tool, although some do overemphasize structure as a cost containment mechanism and miss its possibilities as a weapon of competitive advantage. Unfortunately, too many corporate internal advisors, organization development and human resource professionals, have become caught up in the "structure-is-an-evil-force" school of thought and, as a result, have been of limited value as guides to making the most useful choices about structural forms.

Structure provides a key context for shaping behaviors. For example, how employees are grouped and how these groups are ordered in relation to each other can influence whether new product development flourishes or languishes. Consumer product giant Procter & Gamble has been criticized for letting Olestra, a cholesterol- and calorie-free fat substitute, remain in its research labs for over two decades, far longer than is usually required for a new food ingredient to receive regulatory approval. Why the delay? One former P&G engineer blames the company's rigid organization structure, dominated by the marketing function. The structure reflected P&G's strategy of selling consumer products. Olestra was an ingredient that could be used in many products, but the structure did not easily provide a home or a power base for components; it was geared to accommodate only final products.

Inappropriate groupings of key employees is another problem plaguing many businesses. At General Motors at one point the heads of research and car design reported to a head of R&D, who in turn reported to the executive in charge of GM's data processing and aerospace subsidiaries, both far away from the automobile-making side of the company. This arrangement made it difficult for car designers to work closely with car engineers (who were based in the various auto divisions) to develop new vehicle models, adding to the time and costs required for this key process. Scientists, and their ideas about relevant new technologies, were also kept away from the people most able to apply their discoveries by these reporting relationships. Each managerial interface on an organization chart represents an obstacle to be surmounted, with wall height increasing with the seniority of the manager's title.

Dysfunctional Structures

P&G's product-oriented structure is far from all bad. Over the years it has supported the competitive successes of Crest toothpaste, Tide detergent, and many other well-known consumer brands. But it shares a common characteristic with many organization structures: A close examination of it provides a detailed road map of how the company's past successes were achieved. Most organization structures better represent their companies' histories than their promise. They are a result of old political adjustments and past strategies and are an indicator of who are today's most highly paid employees. They seldom reflect the current basis of competition and almost never provide much of a power base for the critical capabilities upon which the businesses' futures may well depend.

Paul Jacques Grillo, a talented French architect, has observed the same problems in the ways many building are designed. Even though horizontal openings best accommodate the movement of the eyes as they look outward, homes and offices continue to be designed with tall, vertical windows. Why? Because, he says, in the Middle Ages narrow, vertical windows were mandatory. They are an ideal shape from which to aim a bow and arrow or pour boiling oil down on hostile visitors. Though these original defensive needs no longer exist, the design persists. Grillo has also puzzled over the appearance of the typical midwestern farmhouse, usually rising three stories from a vast, flat prairie. While at one time its height might have helped early settlers resist Indian attacks, its main function now seems to be to serve as a clear target for lightning and tornadoes.

Functionality can easily become outdated. This is a problem common to many organization structures. A need may go away, a problem get solved, or a constraint disappear, but the past often lives on in organization charts. The GM situation, concentrating technologists in a separate organization, may have made good sense at a time when technological talent was scarce and in high demand. But this logic is invalid now that the industry has a surplus of this kind of talent and GM faces a competitive situation requiring technological inputs to be widely available throughout the company.

Thriving in a business environment that prizes both focus and the ability to quickly change the focus as new conditions demand requires a new breed of corporation. This "new corporation" will most likely emerge from a deliberate effort to transform the organizational configurations that have worked in the past to those demanded by present reality. This necessitates a head-on confrontation with much of the conventional wisdom about how a company *should* be organized—and then movement beyond it.

In the 1980s and 1990s there has been a paucity of good, creative thinking about organization structure. The field has been in a rut partly because of the tendency, mentioned earlier in this chapter, to discount structure's significance. It has also suffered from the existence of a smokescreen of nonissues and poor, or incomplete, new alternatives.

False Starts

Many hours have been lost, and perhaps too many articles and books written, debating issues such as the pros and cons of centralized and decentralized structures. This is not just one of those "it all depends" issues; it is frequently a misleading concern. All sustainably successful companies are essentially centralized, but—and this is the real trick— they are centralized in a way that can allow for a tremendous degree of local autonomy. It is possible to have your cake and it eat it, too, if careful employee selection and extensive training are done before granting autonomy and if computer-based information systems are used to provide a performance-monitoring safety net. The degree of centralization or decentralization seemingly implied by a particular structure can be a distracting issue.

Also misleading are some of the traditional, tired choices frequently offered when alternative organizational configurations—functional, divisional, or a blend of each (a/k/a matrix)—are considered. When complete organization charts—ones that show all management positions in a company—are examined, they almost always indicate the company is built up from *functionally oriented* work groupings (e.g., sales, manufacturing, finance, human resources). Superimposed on this functional foundation may be some type of divisional structure, most commonly grouping the functions relating to individual products, strategic business units, or geography. In some cases, usually in small, single-product, or excessively centralized companies, the functional groupings of activities persists all the way to the top of the hierarchy. Regardless, this near-inevitable functional dominance in most organizations often makes the choice between functional and divisional structures either meaningless or of limited value. And the choice of a matrix hybrid configuration too frequently covers up the fact that no real choice has been made at all; instead, a structural compromise has been chosen that builds in chronic conflict (instead of conflict resolution) and high coordination costs.

Too often, structures and structural improvements fail because they are only half-steps in the right direction or are based on the management fad of the moment. Teams are often very useful, but they are building blocks of the structure, not the structure itself. Dotted lines on an organization chart and dual reporting relationships, like matrices, usually are substitutes for making choices, rather than indicators of a strong structure.

Some "models" of the corporation of the future are good thought stimulants but weak structural forms. Peter Drucker's vision of the company as a symphony orchestra vividly characterizes the nature of control and coordination that will be required but leaves little room for work not done by well-trained professionals. Charles Handy's creative conceptualization of the "shamrock organization" (he is, after all, the son of a

Church of Ireland archdeacon) represents the fresh thinking so needed about breaking a monolithic work force into core employees, part-time workers, and subcontractors. But this green, cloverlike plant is probably a better national emblem than instrument for focusing on competitive capabilities.

Harvard Business School's D. Quinn Mills has taken the team idea several steps further than most of its popularizers. He advocates forming companies from clusters, groups of people from different disciplines who work together semipermanently. Some of these clusters run businesses that deal directly with customers, some provide support services, others work on change projects, and still others form alliances with outsiders. His ideas, not too dissimilar from the model some consulting and other professional service firms follow to organize themselves, have been applied at companies such as British Petroleum, Du Pont, and General Electric's Canadian operations. But the application generally has been in overhead or staff functions, not throughout the business, probably because the free-flowing nature of the semiautonomous clusters does not allow for the kind of integration required by the revenue-generating parts of these companies.

Other antihierarchists have put their faith in computer systems and communications networks to provide the structural backbone for tomorrow's enterprises. One such view sees the new organization chart looking like "a flat web of departments with direct ties crisscrossing to groups throughout the organization. Management will float above these groups, directing them without cushions of middle managers."

Nice work if you can get it. An intriguing vision, too, but one probably not worth holding one's breath for while waiting for it to materialize. This view, like many held by believers in fluid structures pulled together by information technology, tends to ignore the psychological usefulness of hierarchy and managers. Managers bear more than just information loads. At times they serve as great anxiety and uncertainty buffers, something less easily provided by electronic data bases and computer screens. It is also unclear how this nonstructure will focus resources and direct attention to issues beyond the scope of the hot-wired network.

Notwithstanding these criticisms, there are useful aspects to each of these ideas. The trick is to sift them out, combine them where possible, and compare them with what seems to be working in the real world.

PART ONE
RESIZE

Chapter 2
Start With the Work

Why most downsizings and restructurings fail.

Many—possibly most—downsizings fail.

That is the message conveyed by studies of the aftermath of the wave of global corporate cutbacks that began in the late 1970s. More than half the 135 major U.S. companies that attempted massive restructurings failed to achieve significant increases in their value relative to their competition, reported *The Economist*.

A group of University of Michigan professors spent four years studying the effects of downsizing in thirty automobile industry companies. Among their main observations: White-collar productivity has shown little significant improvement, and administrative costs in many American companies are still far above those of their strongest global competitors.

Problems With Downsizing as a Strategy

Unmet Objectives

A wide-ranging study by a leading actuarial firm found an even bleaker picture than that observed by the Michigan researchers. It asked over 1,000 companies what they had hoped to achieve from their downsizing or cutback efforts. Then they asked the companies if their expectations were met.

The companies' objectives covered a broad range:

- Almost 90 percent wanted to reduce expenses
  —But fewer than half actually did!
- About three quarters hoped for productivity improvements
  —And only 22 percent achieved them.

- More than half wanted to improve cash flow or increase share-holder's return on investment
  —But fewer than 25 percent were able to.
- More than half expected to reduce bureaucracy or speed decision making
  —And only 15 percent did.

Many of these downsizers sought improvements in customer satisfaction and product quality from their reorganizations. Others expected to become more innovative or better able to utilize new technologies. But fewer than 10 percent felt they had met their goals in these key areas.

Corporations commonly streamline operations to improve their competitive position. But only 191 of these 1,000 businesses reported increases in competitive advantage resulting from their downsizings. David Heenan, senior executive of the Hong Kong-based multinational Jardine Matheson, warns that companies shouldn't "expect an organization with anemic headquarters to forge breakthrough strategies."

Cutting Muscle Instead of Fat

Exxon—a rival of Royal Dutch Shell for the accolade of "world's largest oil company"—has had more than its fair share of criticism for the ways it downsized. But its experience has some important lessons for other companies and is worth considering. Some critics have charged that Exxon's shift from a "cradle to grave" to a "lean and mean" company came at the price of cutting muscle as well as fat. Exxon cut R&D expenditures by 20 percent during a period when Shell increased its research spending by almost a third. Nor have Exxon's oil exploration efforts been as aggressive as those of some of its global rivals.

But probably most stinging have been the criticisms Exxon received in the wake of the 1989 *Exxon Valdez* oil spill off the Alaskan coast. The *New York Times* charged that Exxon had responded to that incident in "slow motion" and questioned the extent to which Exxon had been blindsided by the reductions in its headquarters staffing from 1,362 to 320.

Several former Exxon executives claimed the massive cost cutting had made the company more "accident prone." They attributed this in part to overworked survivors of the downsizing and in part to the elimination of a group of oil-spill-response experts who were the repository of much of the company's know-how on this subject. Exxon's top environmental staffer also was moved out of corporate headquarters during the pre-*Valdez* restructuring, a move a now-retired company official felt signaled a weakening of commitment to environmental concerns.

Restructuring's failures also have taken other forms. Some have a more human face.

Human Costs

Harry Levinson, a pioneer in the application of psychological insights to management, has seen many companies "blundering" through the change processes involved in reorganization, merger, and acquisition. He observes: "Early retirements have left many . . . bereft of organization memory. There is much reinventing of the wheel." Levinson also fears that some companies "will never regain the enthusiastic commitment of once loyal employees."

A survey of *Industry Week*'s readers supports Levinson's concerns. Sixty percent of the middle managers polled said they feel less loyalty to their employers than they did five years ago. Many managers who survived large-scale cutbacks have ridden emotional seesaws ever since. First feeling relief and sometimes even elation that they were spared job loss, many soon found this sense of well-being replaced by a combination of guilt and despair. One Georgia-Pacific headquarters manager felt: "I'm obsolete. I'm at a dead end. There's no way up. No way down. And no way out."

A Los Angeles branch manager of a division spun off by Raytheon echoed this concern: "There's very little upward mobility around this company anymore, and I'm out of here as soon as I can land something decent."

Peter Drucker's view of the human aftermath of restructuring is equally as blunt: "The cynicism out there is frightening. Middle managers have become insecure, and they feel unbelievably hurt. They feel like slaves on an auction block."

A manager in a major New York bank became very cynical about the results of the bank's continual reductions of staff. He observed that, while too many good employees were "thrown out on the street," the same top management team that got the bank into all its problems with foreign loans and overreliance on interest-spread income was still in place. He felt that the post-downsizing atmosphere was one in which "instead of trying to get work done, people are constantly covering their ass." His biggest complaint focused on how to deal with the concerns of his subordinates, in the face of the bank's uncertain prospects. "When someone asks you, 'What's my career path?' and you don't have one yourself, what do you say?"

When this manager's comments were reported in a national business magazine, the bank's personnel director quickly wrote a damage control letter to the editor. The director cited evidence from quarterly polls of employee attitudes to show that most middle managers took a favorable view of the restructuring and that, since its occurrence, they found their jobs more fulfilling.

Charges. Countercharges. At times it is difficult to sort reality from perception. One fact is beyond dispute, though. Three years after this exchange, the bank's top management found its competitive position had declined to the point that the bank's best hope for the future was to be acquired by a stronger institution. Now its identity and organization has disappeared—at the cost of several thousand additional lost jobs.

The impact of these human costs has not been lost on the competitors of companies going through retrenchment. Kevin Walsh, an executive vice-president of a bank competing with Chicago-based Continental Bank Corporation, observes: "It's tough for them to keep their morale up when they're going through that kind of restructuring. We try to take full advantage of any signs of weakness like that. We go for the throat."

Continual Downsizing

Some of these adverse human reactions resulted from a boomeranglike effect: Just when you feel you have gotten rid of the problem, it comes back at you, with a vengeance. Too often downsizing only begets more downsizing.

Successive rounds of cutbacks seem to be the fate of many companies in industries such as computers, financial services, and telecommunications. One consultant who studied the aftermath of corporate restructuring in more than 800 companies discovered that almost all the companies surveyed found it necessary to replace some of the people they had dismissed. A quarter of these businesses replaced 10 percent or more.

Chrysler Corporation, a great turnaround success story of the 1980s, illustrates this unfortunate pattern. After reducing its work force by a third in the early 1980s, it allowed staffing levels to balloon by mid decade to the point where they surpassed the preturnaround head count. By the early 1990s a Chrysler executive was forced to admit that the bloat had returned, as he announced the first of a new series of programs to re-reduce white collar jobs.

Some companies tire of repeatedly announcing the "last cutback" and declare themselves in a state of continual downsizing. The message to employees is that their jobs will be, for the foreseeable future, continually at risk. While this might be interpreted as a sign of realism and candor, it is too often a lame excuse for poor planning, suitable only for a business in terminal decline. What company would make similar public projections about its expectations for ongoing market share losses, margin shrinkages, or earnings reductions?

John Whitney, a Columbia business school professor and a leading authority on turnaround management, likes to tell his students there are three stages to the successful revival of a business. First comes the crisis actions that stop the company's hemorrhaging. Then the business must be returned to profitability. Finally, a way needs to be found to grow the company again. The first two of these usually involve deep head count reduction and tight cost control. But these emergency tactics, if kept in place too long, can make it impossible to make the intelligent investments needed to reach stage three. For this stage a different mentality, and possibly a different management, is needed. Otherwise, the once troubled business may find it is good at only one thing: cutting back.

Faulty Assumptions About Reorganization

Behind these statistics and stories are several assumptions about strategy and organization that, at least implicitly, guide many companies' reorganizations. They reinforce the dangerous impact of the conventional wisdom discussed in the Prologue. They are of questionable soundness and have led many businesses into a number of difficulties. Here are the most frequently troublesome:

• *Growth can't be all that bad.* Many companies are addicted to growth, sometimes at the cost of their survival. This is what causes the fat to return. We have overlearned the lesson of economies of scale and have underappreciated how size creates inertia. The most popular basic economics text in use when most American executives studied business told them "large size breeds success, and success further success."

The incentives behind bigness are unmistakable. Psychologically, how many executives of mid-size businesses haven't dreamed of being listed among the Fortune 500? Which Fortune 500 company would prefer not to make the Fortune 50 list? Financially, for chief executives, generally the larger your company, the larger your pay. For middle managers, the larger your department, the larger your paycheck.

Drucker sums up the consequences of these tendencies by maintaining: "A penalty of size is that you try to do everything, and no one can do everything well."

▪ *The best way to deal with unnecessary overhead is by frontal assault.*
When times turn hard for a business, as they always do at some point,
head-on overhead cost reduction is a common first priority. Unfortunately overhead frequently behaves like the hydra—you can cut off one
portion, only to find it quickly grows back. Lasting changes in a company's administrative cost structure require rethinking the basic structure, not just whittling away at its edges.

Too often a great deal of effort is devoted to putting an artificial
value on each component of overhead when what is really needed is a
bottom-up examination of the work processes in place that are generating the need for the overhead in the first place. Overhead activities are
the symptoms, not the disease.

▪ *Clever, quick fixes will solve most problems.* Overhead reduction campaigns are the most commonly attempted quick fix. Early retirement
programs are another. One postmortem analysis of downsizing companies that offered these seemingly attractive early-outs found that 80 percent of the businesses offering them ended up losing good performers,
people they wanted or needed to keep.

Another "creative" approach to payroll reduction is the institution
of a two-tier pay system. Newcomers are paid at a significantly lower
rate for doing the same work as those previously hired. Tightening labor
supplies and work force resentments have limited this tactic's usefulness. This worker resentment factor should not be underestimated.
Some employers have noticed productivity drops on the part of the
lower-paid second-tier workers—drops that often wipe out the cost advantage of the dual system (and bring their effective pay per unit back
up to the first-tier worker's pay rate).

The built-in inequity of this quick fix has caused problems far back
in history. The Roman emperor Macrinus, in 217 A.D., tried something
like this when he reduced salt rations and pay for new recruits but kept
compensation at the old levels for those already on board. This was an
early attempt to solve Rome's budget problems through limited cuts in
military spending. His move caused such dissension among both new
hires and veterans that a mutiny ensued, and the soldiers killed Macrinus.

Pay concessions, which have their place as a tactic to cope with temporary emergencies, can also backfire when they are used to cope with
a long-term decline in competitiveness. One American company attempted to obtain a 40 percent wage cut from its factory workers. The
goal: to bring costs closer to those of its Asian competition. As happened
in Rome, the workers revolted, and the company suffered a long strike

to achieve what ended up as a 10 percent pay reduction. The strategic significance of the lower payroll was, however, much less. In this company, as in many manufacturers, direct labor accounted for 15 percent of the total value added. So the company's net cost saving: only 1.5 percent, achieved at the expense of significantly deteriorated relations with the employees upon whom the company's future competitiveness depended.

▪ *The place to start is head count reduction.* Almost everybody does this. Downsizing, rightsizing, streamlining, and restructuring are all euphemisms for reducing the size of the work force. It is an agonizing, painful process, an emotional "hot potato" that most companies try to get behind them as quickly as possible—and, judging from the studies and examples cited, one that is not producing—even at very high cost—the benefits promised.

It is a problem not limited to the private sector. When the chiefs of the U.S. Army, Air Force, Navy, and Marines sent their spending goals for the 1990s to then Secretary of Defense Richard Cheney, each military service anticipated significant staffing reductions. But the assumptions behind their plans showed they were still oriented around the mission of the Cold War, rather than the new challenges of the decade.

On a more micro level, downsizing is a trap that many Japanese companies have avoided. They avoid confusing *cost cutting* with *head count reduction.* Consider how they manage the development of a new product. The Japanese predetermine the product's cost—on the basis of the price they feel customers will accept, not on their thick library of manuals of historical costs—before even thinking about how they will make it. Then they use this target cost as the reference point to influence the efforts of their product developers, manufacturing engineers, and suppliers. In short, they take what many Western companies assume is an *effect* and make it a *cause.* This process ensures that products are designed to be as inexpensive as possible and that the methods used to make them are as economical as possible.

Contrast this with the typical European and American approach to price setting that starts with microscopic measurement of the anticipated labor hours a new product will require (already focusing attention on head count). Added to this is a formula-determined amount for overhead and administrative charges. This number is finally massaged with a profit margin computation based on the stock market's current expectation of the company's return on investment. All these convolutions and financial abstractions make it very difficult for a manager proposing a new product to get a feel for what is actually making the product cost what the numbers say it will. (Is the manufacturing process the right one? Do we have too many steps in the logistics pipeline? Do we need so many progress reports so frequently?) And without this feel, it is very difficult to figure out what to do to reduce the product's costs—other than to go after staffing levels.

Head counts are vulnerable because they are very visible in the accounting systems many Western businesses use. But not all non-Japanese companies have fallen into this trap. James Bryant, a vice-president at medical equipment maker Baxter International, focuses his efforts on costs, not head count. His philosophy is one of adding people if the net result of their efforts is reduced expenses. This logic is acknowledged by many managers, but practiced by too few.

Minnesota Mining and Manufacturing has also avoided these missteps. It has managed to avoid layoffs of its almost 90,000 worldwide employees while, over a five-year period, reducing labor and manufacturing costs by 35 percent. How did 3M accomplish this difficult balancing act? With clear, consistent leadership from its chief executive and the willingness to *spend* money to *save* money on such items as new plant layouts, automation, and just-in-time inventory methods. These cost reductions have also helped 3M protect its future. 3M's research budgets, from which its new product introductions flow, are twice U.S. industry averages, a generosity made possible in recessionary times by close watch on costs more peripheral to the core of the company.

Resizing the Right Things

What went wrong? Why have positive gains from organization restructuring been so hard to realize? Primarily because *too much attention has been focused on eliminating unnecessary jobs, and too little on cutting unnecessary work.* The importance of outplacing people has been learned, but not the techniques of outplacing work. One downsizing survivor lamented: "We cut the work force, but left all the work and the old ways of doing things in place."

A recent review of several hundred companies that downsized found that fewer than half of them took steps to identify and rid themselves of low-value work. This approach puts these companies under tremendous pressure to restaff once their immediate economic pressure lets up. And in the interim, it puts the employees who survive the cutbacks under tremendous pressure to cope with the unchanged workload. This also helps explain the missed objectives of the 1,000 companies mentioned at the start of this chapter; only half actually achieved lasting cost savings, and only a third noticed productivity improvements.

Perhaps this is a good point to bring in the perspective of the architect, our role model for the organizational planner of the future.

Many modern architects have adopted Louis Sullivan's famous dictum: "Form follows function." Their analysis might suggest that a bloated form is really just a *symptom of excess functionality*. And excess functionality is a result of doing, or attempting to do, too much.

In the Prologue, I stressed the importance of restructuring companies by changing their architecture. Building bridges and lowering walls are some of the keys to this new architecture. The architect of these structures might ask, if these changes are among the most necessary, does it not make the most economic sense first to consider the possibilities of:

- Reducing the area that needs to be enclosed?
- Minimizing the distances that need to be bridged?

Too often companies—and their management consultants—develop elaborate organizational solutions when they might have been better advised to reconsider the nature of the problem: What is the work that really needs to happen? And how? And where? And by whom?

Then comes the hard part, the resizing. Picasso is credited with saying: "Every act of creation is first of all an act of destruction." The famed economist Joseph Schumpeter espoused a view of the successful enterprise as one that "incessantly revolutionizes the economic structure from within, incessantly destroying the old one, incessantly creating the new one." The trick here is to plan the movement from old to new in a way that does not lead to mindless destruction and chaos. Which means starting out with a clear idea of where to end up.

What Stays, What Goes?

How do you know high-value work when you see it? This is one of those questions (like the favorite of the strategy planner: "What business are you really in?") that is easy to pose and often extremely difficult to answer. A good place to start, though, is by viewing your company from more than one vantage point as you consider resizing its turf.

At times during the design process architects stand back from their detailed drawings and look at the structure they are planning as a whole, as might a bystander walking by. They focus on it in relation to its site, how well it fits—should more earth be moved to make way for the building, or should the building's design be modified to accommodate some unique feature of the terrain?

At other points in their planning, they try to understand what they are doing from the inside out. How will the space be perceived by those using it? Will the floor plan of the new office building help or hinder the work done by those who will occupy it? Without the benefit of these *shifts in perspective*, the architect might design a functionless beauty or an efficient eyesore.

Similarly, dual perspectives are essential when planning the restructuring of a corporation. Many reorganization efforts flounder because they take an excessively simpleminded view of the enterprise's work.

One useful perspective is the "big picture," the view from the top of the corporate hierarchy looking down. Analysis of this macro view can help sort out which parts of the business are central to competitive success, which tangential, and which out-and-out hindrances.

This big picture—after some degree of editing—then needs to be complemented by a bottom-of-the-hierarchy-up examination of what is being done and where and how. This microperspective will also provide the organization planner with a number of targets for resizing.

Chapters 3 and 4 consider these two perspectives. I start with the macro view; there is no point fine-tuning something that really should be discarded.

Chapter 3
Look From the Top Down

Companies are portfolios of skills and capabilities. Resources should be concentrated on those providing the greatest competitive advantage.

What you see when you look at a corporation depends on where you sit. If your home base is in marketing, you may see the company as a collection of products and brands, each aimed at a particular customer segment. If you have a manufacturing orientation, the company appears more like a cluster of plants and facilities, each containing discrete processes and work flows, all linked by a logistics network. From a financial perspective, the working reality is that of a portfolio of asset groupings, each providing—you hope—a targeted return to the extent revenues exceed costs.

A human resources-oriented view might first see the company as composed of populations of employees, perhaps grouped in several castes—e.g., salaried, hourly, part-time. A more sophisticated examination could center on the talents and skills of these people, quality instead of quantity. And a future-oriented view may see the company as a series of career paths and an emerging mix of shortages and surpluses of talent.

These differing big pictures are all "correct," but limiting. Each leaves out more than it includes. They all lack a "helicopterlike" perspective on the business as a whole, the view supposedly attainable only from the top of the corporate hierarchy.

The View From the Top

Consider the chief executive's perspective. When a CEO looks at the company, several features stand out most sharply. These are the traditional components of corporate structure: divisions, functional departments, strategic business units (SBUs), and subsidiaries. They are the activities over which the chief executive has responsibility. They form the mental model the top leadership has of the business. Most companies take these components for granted as their basic subunits.

Unfortunately, these components cloud more than clarify the perspective most essential to the intelligent resizing of a company's work.

When changes are made in a company's strategy, or when changes outside its control make readjustment or retrenchment necessary, the lines and boxes on the company's organization chart are also frequently shifted. These moves usually seem to make good sense at the time—form just following function, after all—but as the retrospective research cited in Chapter 2 indicates, moving the boxes and redrawing the lines do not always pay off.

This happens because, frequently, the wrong question is being asked. The search is usually for the "best" organizational configuration: flat, functional, divisional, matrix, or some hybrid. This issue, which eventually does need to be addressed (and will be in Chapter 7), is premature if it is the first thing that comes to mind when considering the company as a whole. It diverts attention from careful consideration of the "functionality" that the "form" is being adapted to. It also makes the company susceptible to the management fad of the moment, so that a *means* becomes the *goal*: How can we flatten our structure, use cross-departmental teams, or become an information-based organization? These are all potentially useful *tactics*, but for what *end*?

This type of reorganization, driven from the top down, is one that deals with the *structures* for doing things, rather than the *things* that need doing. Its view of the boxes on the organization chart too often goes no deeper than the head count the boxes contain. This perspective is troublesome and can be misleading, but even more dangerous is the viewpoint provided by some contemporary forms of strategic planning.

Top Management—Prisoners of Outdated Strategic Planning?

Since the late 1970s, the view from the top of most corporations has been strongly influenced by their leaders' planning doctrine. Executives have been taught, by both consultants and business schools, that the best way to plan for a complex company's long-term future is by breaking the company into discrete components, called strategic business units (SBUs). For a time this practice provided a helpful way to unbundle the corporation and to select strategies most appropriate to each unit's individual situation.

Companies were, according to SBU-adherents, best thought of as a portfolio of individual businesses: some brand-new and unproven, some growing rapidly and consuming great amounts of cash, some (if you were lucky) growing less rapidly and generating the cash needed by the up-and-comers, and some out-and-out losers.

Strategic planners eventually carried the idea one step further. They developed formulas that appeared to identify the contribution each business unit was making to the company's overall stock price. Called value-based planning (as in shareholder value), its application, along with techniques such as junk-bond-driven leveraged buyouts, helped deconglomerate many corporate dinosaurs in the financial go-go years of the 1980s.

These planning techniques are both logical and quantifiable, descriptive as well as prescriptive. They provide a seemingly attractive way for the head of an enterprise to put arms around what might have become an increasingly diverse array of businesses. But thinking of a corporation as if it were similar to a portfolio of stocks or other investments can also be very limiting and one-dimensional.

This kind of thinking tends to overemphasize the uniqueness of each business and often assumes that all the competition in which the corporation is engaged occurs when its business units do battle with their counterparts in other companies. It suggests that the role of top corporate management is either secondary or passive with regard to competition. It also implies that top management's role is primarily that of a banker to the individual SBU, concerned chiefly with financial resource allocation, and that it adds value mainly through "balancing the portfolio" by buying or selling the SBUs that make up the company.

This approach encourages a "trader's mentality" on the part of top management. Traders like to buy and sell, conglomerate and deconglomerate. But they do not know very much about how to grow the company from within.

Decentralization, sometimes extreme decentralization, is also encouraged, because each business is expected to stand on its own, containing most of the resources it needs for its operations. This simplifies the job of top management (it has only to focus on each SBU's bottom line and consider the details of its operations on an exception-only basis).

But this simplification comes at a great cost. Stressing stand-alone uniqueness and managing through the blinders of short-term earnings results in living, growing business entities treated almost as if they were fragments of the company's stock certificate. The disease of the stock markets—perspective that seldom extends beyond next quarter's financials—is passed along to the company.

There is another danger when the SBU framework dominates corporate decision making. This is the tendency to grow redundant resources in the company as each SBU, over time, builds up all the functions and staffing it feels it needs to operate as autonomously as possible. At times headquarters management tries to check the emergence of this costly duplication by mandating resource sharing across SBUs, by using central service groups, or both. But these well-meaning attempts at cost containment send mixed signals to the SBUs ("I thought this company believed in decentralization and that we were supposed to be running our own business"), and they also can impose heavy coordination costs in terms of time and loss of flexibility.

Problems can arise regarding competitiveness as well as costs. In the late 1980s Great Britain's National Economic Office became concerned about the slow growth of the United Kingdom's leading electronic corporations. During a time of rapid global market expansion, they received far less than their fair share of the new business. After some study, the Office identified the primary culprit as the tendency of many of these companies to subdivide themselves into small business units, each with assumed freedom to chart an independent course. Rather than the expected release of entrepreneurial energy, these subdivisions tended to take a more narrow view of global opportunities than did their corporate parents and oriented themselves to delivering short-term performance by selling existing products in existing markets.

How were so many otherwise intelligently managed companies led down these paths? They took a seemingly attractive shortcut in their thinking. *They confused a framework for planning with a basis for organizing power and resources.* They used a perspective that directs top management's attention to the financial scorekeeping aspects of the business at the cost of neglecting the underlying mechanisms that create value for their customers.

What Should You See When Looking From the Top Down?

Recent strategic planning doctrine is attempting to move away from its deal-driven mentality. Some executives are taking a "back to the basics" approach, asking the traditional first question of business planning: *What business are we really in?* This is the question that was supposed to have saved the American railroads, according to conventional business school wisdom. Had they only made it the core of their business planning efforts in the first half of the twentieth century, they would have realized they were really in the transportation business, not just the railroad industry. Then, hindsighters say, they would have quickly diversified into aviation and trucking and never suffered losses of market share to these competitors.

Maybe so, but a number of railroads—in America, Asia, and Europe—are well positioned to enter the twenty-first century as economically strong carriers that have strayed very little from the traditional definition of a railroad. But they *have* applied a measure of creativity and innovation to this definition and developed new means of moving people—such as the French high-speed TGV and the Japanese bullet trains—and goods—for example, the computer-driven, centrally controlled Union Pacific. And other companies that have tried to broaden the definition of the industry they are in have found themselves owning a string of essentially unrelated businesses that are hard to manage centrally.

Michael Porter, Harvard Business School professor and author of several of the core texts on strategic planning, suggests companies move beyond this expanding-the-big-picture view and look instead at the key components of a business and how they are interrelated. He calls these relationships a company's "value chain." Porter views every company as a collection of activities that either design, make, market, deliver, or in some way support its products. He suggests that companies carefully measure the cost of each activity and understand which activities add the most to the value customers receive from the products. This is a good way to examine microscopically the components of a business. However, just as the "what business are we really in?" method is too broad, Porter's popular approach can be narrowly applied in ways that miss what it is that a business is best at.

Traditional value chain analysis provides a function-by-function view of what a company really is. This perspective is helpful in identifying places where money is being spent and costs need to be cut, but less so when you are trying to get a fix on what a company's unique strengths are. These strengths frequently relate more to the ways functional competences are blended than to the specifics of a company's marketing operation or financial control system.

Competences and Capabilities: A New Paradigm

To overcome the limitations and unneeded baggage inherent in conventional strategic planning, several leading companies are experimenting with a new approach to managing their future. They are organizing their development around what they call *core competences* or *capabilities*. Instead of asking the static "What business are we really in?" question, they probe more deeply by considering: "What special skills and know-how do we bring to the businesses we are *now* in that can serve as a foundation upon which *future* businesses can be built?"

Over time, in addition to acquiring cash and physical assets, many companies build a stock of distinctive competences. These skills result from the adaptations the business makes in response to the demands of customers and the challenges of competitors. Because each company's history is unique, so is its profile of competences, although, taken individually, many of these capacities may be generic or common. In some ways, this profile is the corporate equivalent of character or personality.

These are not new ideas. Philip Selznik articulated many of these when he worked at the RAND Corporation in the 1950s. More recently they have been elaborated on and championed by a pair of professors of corporate strategy: India-born C. K. Prahalad and London-based Gary Hamel. Their work is based, in part, on research into the factors behind the global competitive successes of several major Japanese corporations.

Prahalad and Hamel credit a reasonable portion of Japanese success to the stumbles of many North American and European companies. They argue: "It is not very comforting to think that the essence of Western strategic thought can be reduced to eight rules for excellence, seven S's, five competitive forces, four product-life cycle stages, three generic strategies, and innumerable two-by-two matrices." They notice that these—and other planning concepts such as product life cycles, experience curves, and business portfolios—often have a number of "toxic side effects."

These older planning concepts, Prahalad and Hamel say, yield predictable strategies, easy for competitors to decode, and create preferences for selling rather than building businesses on the part of short-term-oriented practitioners. The application of many of these mechanistic methods can have the result, over time, of grinding down a business. They concentrate executive talent on trimming ambitions, on limiting expenditures to those that support the logic dictated by whatever planning concept is in vogue. Such force-fitting and overapplication of financial return hurdles divert top management attention from what Prahalad and Hamel's research finds to be the real sources of competitive advantage: the ability to make better use of existing resources to reach goals that would otherwise be unattainable.

Prahalad and Hamel suggest there is more mileage to be gained by thinking of a company as a portfolio of potentially reinforcing competences than by viewing it as a collection of stand-alone businesses. This is not a static view. It suggests that creating a business that is successful today is only half the battle. What is most significant for the company's long-term health is the nurturing and leveraging of current sources of advantage so they will have a greater payoff tomorrow.

Where are these sources of advantage, of added value, to be found? They are embedded within a company's products. They are "carried" in the skills and know-how of its workers and managers. Prahalad and Hamel call them the collective learning of the corporation. They are the capabilities in which a business excels and that its customers prize.

For Sony these capabilities might involve miniaturization and select electronic technologies. At Canon, key capabilities range from fine optics to precision mechanics and also include microelectronics. Honda has evolved a string of businesses—from motorcycles and autos to lawn mowers, power generators, and boat engines—from its central focus on building high-speed, lightweight engines. And it continually sharpens this focus through the know-how it obtains competing in racing events that seemingly have little to do with the products it sells.

Focusing a company around its significant capabilities is not a skill limited to the Japanese, though. Motorola, an American leader in the application of quality improvement techniques, is careful not to let its successful product line drive its self-image. It organizes its activities around an *overall objective* to be the world leader in wireless communications, the capability that underlies its businesses in portable phones and pagers. By not limiting itself to the communication by radio of the spoken word, it has leveraged its wireless communication skills to guide development of products that create computer networks without wires and help travelers navigate using satellite transmissions.

This kind of thinking encourages Motorola to plan for its future by anticipating the uses its customers will make of the products it *could* create from its capabilities. One such vision making the rounds at Motorola involves planning for the communications products necessary to permit telephone numbers to be assigned to people, rather than fixed locations, such as homes and offices. It is doubtful this flight of imagination would have emerged if the company's assets and management practices had been focused primarily on making money from paging devices and radiophones.

Rubbermaid is another example of the relatively few American-based companies that have learned this art of serendipitous exploitation. When one of its executives toured a Rubbermaid plant that used plastic blow-molding techniques to produce picnic coolers, he realized that the same know-how could be used in the division that made furniture. Soon, the company released the first units of its WorkManager System, a collection of lightweight, durable, and low-price office furniture. This system eventually came to account for more than half of the division's total sales, revenues that never would have materialized if Rubbermaid had not laid out paths to transfer knowledge easily from one business to another.

Driving corporate strategy through this kind of creative insight is still more common in Japanese than in Western businesses. Perhaps walks by executives of one division through another division's manufacturing facilities are less common than they should be. Or perhaps the barriers erected in the name of autonomy and decentralization have eliminated the possibility of synergy and shared common purpose.

Not so, though, at the Japanese company Kao. It drives its growth through a corporatewide focus on ways to coat the surface of materials. This has led it to seemingly divergent businesses, some as mundane as soaps and some as advanced as computer floppy disks. Divergent, though, only to those who miss the underlying common capability—a capability that has also moved the company into the cosmetics business. After all, is not a valued property of makeup its ability to adhere to a material, that is, skin? Ajinomoto, a major Japanese food producer, is another example. In a land where sake and soy sauce are dietary staples, a food products company would be hard pressed not to know something about fermentation techniques. Ajinomoto does, and it has used this know-how to grow the company by making an elastic paper that is used in Sony's better headphones.

The Hard and the Soft Sides of Capabilities

The concept of capabilities is broader than that of technologies. It has both a hard and a soft dimension. Its firm and tangible aspect is its mechanistic side—*what a company is especially good at* (be it miniaturization, making lightweight engines, allowing communications without wires, molding plastics, or coating surfaces). The less tangible but more telling dimension of a capability is the company's *ability to apply its know-how*. Too many companies enshrine potentially significant competences in their R&D departments but lack the mechanisms to move those competences forward into their product lines. Or they may have a successful array of capability-driven products in one division but lack the incentives and mechanisms to utilize their know-how to serve the customers of their other divisions.

The soft dimension is dynamic; its presence and strength determine how able a company is at exploiting its own internal strengths. It is what drives the capabilities' growth and evolution. Companies with unidimensional, mechanistic-only capabilities soon find the value of these competences diminished as they die of old age or are copied or forgotten.

Capabilities form the nucleus of the new corporation. Putting in place the organizational architecture that will allow them to drive the business is the subject of the rest of this book. Here, though, the key issue is to recognize capabilities as the basis around which a business should be sized and to eliminate the capability clutter that occurs over time in most organizations.

What Capabilities Really Count?

For Prahalad and Hamel, the bottom line of their global competitiveness research is simply put: "An organization's capacity to improve existing skills and learn new ones is the most defensible competitive advantage of all." Very true, but not all competences and skills are created equal. Not all are worth improving; resource and time constraints limit how many new ones can be acquired. Companies, even small and medium-size ones, have hundreds of capabilities. Some have thousands. Which ones really count and should be the basis for organizing and resizing, and which can be safely deemphasized or ignored?

Answering these questions requires disaggregation of the competences concept. If competences are to be a useful guide to resizing, it is necessary to analyze a company's capabilities beyond deciding which are "core" and which are not. One way to do this is to use *criticality* to the customer as the yardstick. (See Figure 5.)

Least critical to the customer, as well as least noticed, are the competences, called *complementary capabilities*, that underlie a business's internal support services. These include the administrative activities performed by groups such as the personnel department, the mailroom, the materials management function, the accountants who prepare monthly financial reports, and so on. Necessary as most of these services may be, they are instances of the company doing business with itself, rather than with paying outsiders. Often the most important direct impact of these activities on customers is their cost, which is reflected in the company's overhead and passed along in its prices.

For many manufacturers, *delivery* of the completed product is of secondary importance to compared *production*. Their outbound logistics are among their complementary capabilities and are frequently provided by contractors. Not so for Domino's Pizza. Receiving a fresh-baked pizza within thirty minutes of placing an order is a key value perceived by Domino's customers. This delivery capability is central to Domino's part-production, part-service business.

Figure 5. Four types of capabilities.

Type	Role
1. Cutting edge	Sources of tomorrow's competitiveness
2. Critical	What provide today's competitive advantage
3. Core	Skills common to most companies in a particular business
4. Complementary	Support services, instances of a company doing business with itself

Competences that directly make possible the products or services customers buy are more important than those that just support or complement their provision. There are two types of such competences. *Core capabilities*, in this terminology, are those that are vital to what is being done but that are not unique to any one company. At Domino's, the generic ability to produce pizzas quickly is such a capability. For an airline, these competences may include the abilities to fly planes and to keep them well maintained. They are competences that are often noticed only by their absence—the tray table that never managed to stay latched on your recent flight aboard a financially troubled air carrier, or the pizza that arrived soggy or undercooked.

Critical capabilities are more noticeable, in a positive sense. In fact, they are the keys to achieving competitive distinction. While core capabilities are mature and ordinary, critical capabilities are novel and sources of growth. To paraphrase Alan Kay, Apple Computer's visionary product planner: Critical capabilities are what weren't around when you started your career. You do not take them for granted. At your airline seat, they are the personal video screens that allow you to select whatever combination of movies and video games will best provide diversion on a long flight to Tokyo. At home, it's the appearance of a fresh, hot pizza in less than half an hour from the time you ordered it. In the hands of a Frito-Lay delivery person restocking potato chips in a supermarket, it's the information power available in the hand-held computer that analyzes past purchasing patterns and suggests how many of each flavor of chip to leave behind to maximize next week's sales.

Most critical to future customer needs are the capabilities resident in a business but nascent in the marketplace. These *cutting-edge capabilities* will be embedded in tomorrow's products. Today they may be in the R&D labs, scattered throughout the business, or forgotten in a subsidiary or branch office. Or they may be hard at work in another company in another industry, awaiting transfer to yours. All of which is not to say they are unimportant, just unrecognized.

Capabilities as Dynamic Properties

Capabilities are not static possessions. What might be a critical capability at one point in time, such as Pan American's jet-powered transatlantic fleet was in the 1960s, may lose its differentiating ability as it is imitated by others. Some capabilities, like the mix of factors that contribute to Delta Airline's legendary reputation for friendly and attentive customer service, are harder to imitate. In Delta's case, they result from a blend of competences in employee relations, cross-training, internal communications, staffing from within, and ongoing maintenance of a one-family culture. These are part of a carefully orchestrated management system, self-reinforcing, and built up over a long period of time. It is difficult for a competitor to extract and duplicate any one element of it and expect to rival Delta's overall performance in this area.

What may have been a complementary capability in the past—as information and data processing systems were for airlines when they operated in a completely regulated marketplace—can gain critical importance as the business environment changes. In the deregulated U.S. airline industry, as many as 10,000 fares may change each day. For an air carrier, keeping up with competitors' prices and adjusting its own to maximize the number of seats sold are competitive necessities; these complementary capabilities have become critical.

Sources of Future Growth

The identification and the classification of a corporation's capabilities are not ends in themselves, but a platform for creative insight into ways the business might grow. An example of this is the thinking behind a U.S. Navy unit's long-range planning.

The Naval Aviation Depot Corporation repairs military aircraft—their engines and other related components. It also provides engineering and logistical support for naval aircraft wherever they are based around the world. An early government adopter of private sector practices, such as total quality management and productivity gain sharing, this military agency has also stayed abreast of the latest thinking in strategic planning.

When the U.S. military budget cutbacks began in the early 1990s, the Depot Corporation responded with a forward-looking plan. Realizing the demand for its core capability, aircraft maintenance, would shrink with a smaller post-Cold War fleet and fewer naval aircraft, it decided to give more attention to developing one of its critical capabilities: the manufacture of aircraft parts no longer in production or otherwise available from civilian defense contractors.

This long-present but underemphasized competence became a centerpiece of the Depot Corporation's new plan. While the lessening of global military tensions would predictably translate into less frequent introductions of new aircraft models, the old models would be expected to last longer and to remain current with advances in aviation technologies. This new emphasis on rebuilding, rather than on replacing, could lead to a healthy, long-term business updating components, making avionics smarter, and modifying the long-service aircraft to serve as platforms for the weapons systems of the twenty-first century. The Depot Corporation's past manufacturing competences provided a base from which it could adapt to the needs of the new military and convert a glass that otherwise would have seemed half-empty into one half-full.

Two business school professors, Stanley Davis and William Davidson, speculate that this type of "out-of-the-mainstream" capability-driven growth will become increasingly common. They see car builders in down markets making more money from financing autos than from making them. They anticipate that some airlines may make more money from fees generated by their reservation systems than from flying passengers, and some retailers may earn more from selling customer lists than from selling directly to these customers. Already, some sports clubs are making less money from playing the game than from selling the television rights to those games, and some of Sears Roebuck's strongest businesses have been its financial services subsidiaries, not its stores.

Two Ways Companies Can Grow

A diversified company can grow in either of two ways. First, the businesses under its corporate umbrella can individually and independently expand. This can certainly be useful, but in the long term the added diversity it will create and the difficulties the top executives will have intelligently managing the expanded divisions will produce strong centrifugal forces. Putting in place management systems to rein in these forces adds to the company's overhead, slows down its reaction time to customer requests and competitor moves, and eventually leads to economic decline. This is the kind of growth that the junk-bond-fueled, leveraged-buyout wave of the 1980s arose to correct.

Alternatively, businesses can direct their growth the way many mutually dependent biological organisms do: through creative interplay, or peaceful coexistence. Some of the growth of each business will be driven by the direction provided by its customers, markets, and unique capabilities. But a significant portion will be *propelled by capabilities shared with other businesses within the company.* This is growth as practiced by Ajinomoto, Honda, Motorola, and Rubbermaid. This kind of growth, harder to manage than the first, has the advantage of continuously reinforcing itself. The forces it produces are centripetal, directed back toward the central capabilities.

When you consider these growth-inducing capabilities, you realize there are really just two kinds of companies: focused and unfocused.

Focusing on Competences and Capabilities

Focused companies keenly appreciate the full range of their relevant capabilities, their differing roles, and their dynamics. Their capability repertoire matches the current and emerging needs of their customers. Investment decisions are not made on a stand-alone, project-by-project basis or by relying only on narrow and simplistic yardsticks, such as net present value and return on assets. Instead, priority is given to investments that strengthen critical capabilities that will, in turn, provide returns leveraged through all the products and businesses that can make use of them.

The top management in focused companies has a logic behind its decision making that ties the capabilities together. There is an apparent overall theme to the company. It is rooted in the concrete reality of its key competences, not in fantasy-based wishful thinking freshly manufactured by the company's image handlers. You know when such a theme is in place because its presence forces top management to make difficult choices about which businesses to be in.

And there can be quite an upside to a focused company. Two-thirds of Germany's gross national product is produced by small and mid-size companies with fewer than 1,000 employees each. They account for

about a third of the exports in a country that has become the world's
biggest exporter. These companies and some of their slightly larger
cousins, a group called the *mittelstand*, have collectively grown big by
thinking small. They are paragons of focus.

Many *mittelstand* companies are world leaders in their markets, often with market shares many times larger than those of their nearest
competitor. They prefer to be big fish in small ponds, carefully targeting
the most profitable global market segments and focusing their capabilities on very specific customer requirements.

Outside their niches, most of these companies are unknowns, with
names such as Zuleeg, Panther, and Silberstand. Within their realms,
though, they are often the preferred provider. Zuleeg, a Bavarian textile
maker, is frequently chosen to produce fabrics for many of the world's
best fashion designers. The company is chosen over lower-cost Asian
resources because of the quality it provides through its beyond-the-
state-of-the-art technology. Silberstand, which corrects sound distortion
in the high-fidelity loudspeakers it makes by incorporating a calculator
into each speaker, manages to sell quite a few units in Japan, home of
the leading consumer electronics builders.

What makes these companies so effective? One study, conducted
by a German university, compared them to many of the larger, "brand
name" German multinationals. It found that the overall orientation of
most of the global giants was dominated either by the power of their
technologies or by the demands of their markets. But the mid-size companies did a much better job balancing these two competing orienta-
tions. *Mittelstand* members tend to be both technology and marketing
companies. Their Teutonic origins provide an ample share of technical
and engineering know-how. But their focus and relatively small size
force them to track their customers' needs closely. In these companies
there is no department or employee who is very far away from direct
customer contact. The percentage of employees with intimate knowledge of customer needs is several times higher than it is in larger companies. This market awareness, coupled with technical strengths, has
made many of these businesses unbeatable global competitors.

The United States has its counterparts to the *mittelstand* companies,
such as writing instrument maker A. T. Cross, and the WD-40 Company, the formulator of a ubiquitous multipurpose lubricant. Both
sharply focused companies enjoy superior worldwide reputations.

P. H. Glatfelter, a Pennsylvania papermaker, is another global competitor. It enjoys twice the profit margins of larger paper companies,
three times their average annual return on equity, but only half their
sales growth. In what for larger players is by definition a commodity

business, Glatfelter has cherry-picked to find the more profitable market segments. Explains its chief executive, Thomas Norris: "We've picked and chosen the markets we can service best, and we service the hell out of them." Norris differentiates his company from its competitors by emphasizing a critical capability (customer service) whose profitable use is made possible by limiting the focus of Glatfelter's core capability (paper-making).

For many *mittelstand* companies, their medium size works to their advantage. But what about larger American companies? Are they also able to benefit by channeling their skills?

Some are. When David Johnson left his job as chief executive of baby food maker Gerber Products to head Campbell Soup, he took over a company divided against itself. His predecessor had fragmented the company into forty business units, each self-contained and responsible for everything from inventing new products to making, selling, and shipping them. While many unit managers enjoyed the diversity of their jobs, at times chaos reigned. At one point, the soup business ran a joint promotion tied to a product of Nabisco, even though that Nabisco product competed directly with one made by another Campbell unit. The walls dividing Campbell's businesses had grown higher than those separating the company from its marketplace competitors! And the financial results, not surprisingly, were only half the industry average.

Johnson applied the traditional turnaround medicine: twenty plants were closed and hundreds of headquarters jobs eliminated. He also took an in-depth look at the company's basic capabilities and how they were, or were not, interrelated. This examination drove many of the decisions about the resizing that followed. Johnson narrowed Campbell's focus to embrace what he called two primary building blocks: heat-processed foods and frozen foods. Capability-building was to occur in these two realms. Products that relied on divergent skills—refrigerated fresh dinners, meal services, salmon fishing, and premade salads—became part of Campbell's heritage.

Kodak and Polaroid are also working hard to unblur their strategic images. Kodak has had a fifteen-year string of business mishaps in many hoped-for growth areas: instant photography, batteries, disc cameras, copiers, and printers. Its strong base business, film making, has also lost market share to a Japanese rival, Fuji. As part of an intense effort to demonstrate that Kodak is not a "sleeping giant," its chief executive is focusing Kodak's resources to keep it centered on being an "imaging company"—one highly skilled at making products that process and convert images. This focus is further refined to include only the capabilities that produce photo-quality images. Ruled out are electronic cameras and similar digital technology devices, strongholds of competitors such as Canon and Sony.

Where should Kodak's electronics-oriented technologists go to look for work? At Polaroid, perhaps. This pioneer of instant photography is also recovering from a series of new-product disappointments by sharpening its focus—but in the opposite direction from Kodak. After an anaylsis of its key capabilities, Polariod is actively shifting its mix of staff know-how away from chemistry and toward electronics.

Losing Focus—A Threat to Survival

There are a number of ways companies can lose focus.

Some simply attempt to manage too many capabilities. This can easily occur over time in successful companies—global giants and smaller— that do not actively chart out and manage their competences over their life cycles.

Others dissipate their focus by managing competing competences. Capabilities compete internally for money and talent. They also compete for "share of mind" of top executives—the ability to dominate their mind-set about their customer's needs and how they can best be met. Many companies lack the blended perspective achieved by a number of the *mittelstand* businesses. They become too production-oriented, or too market-driven, or too much like a seesaw, continuously changing from one orientation to another. They forget that a skill or technique does not become a capability until its value is customer-recognized.

The balance between capabilities that directly serve outside customers and those that serve internal needs can be lost. While complementary capabilities are of varying degrees of importance to customers, they are all potential drags on how sharply a corporation is focused.

Companies may also overemphasize core capabilities, diverting attention and resources from capabilities that provide real competitive advantage (the critical capabilities) or reducing the funds available to nurture promising cutting-edge capabilities.

Attention also should be paid to the risk of overinvesting in sources of potential future earnings. More than one company has gone bankrupt, or disappeared in a merger, with a surplus of good but too-far-ahead-of-their-time ideas.

Balancing the capability portfolio seems to be a key to long-term survival and prosperity. In recent years, companies in a variety of industries have either lost their core or allowed it to become rusty as they overemphasized more exciting critical capabilities. This problem plagued many American banks that tried to transform themselves from traditional loan making organizations to broadly diversified "financial supermarkets." Siemens, the German-based global electrical giant, paid a billion-dollar penalty as its cost of reentering the business of producing computer memory chips, components it needed to stay competitive in the computer business. Memory chip know-how was too important to its success to be restructured away.

Involving the Organization Designer in Planning the Strategy

Looking at a company from the top down is a lot like the builder's site selection process. Choices are made about the most promising strategic turf on which to compete, the most favorable ground being one on which capabilities can be marshaled, customers pleased, and competitors kept at bay.

Choosing a place to build is the key decision that must be made before an architect can start planning for a new structure. Frequently the site has been preselected, and the architect must work with or around its characteristics. Seldom can they be ignored. At times, though, the architect is involved in the location choice. This increases the possibility that the building's design will optimally fit its surroundings, as happened at Frank Lloyd Wright's prizewinning house, Fallingwater, or Louis Kahn's Salk Institute on the Pacific coast.

Likewise, organization architects have a vital role to play in helping define a corporation's functionality, helping identify its "strategic turf." Bringing their design talents to bear on the identification and focusing of competitive capabilities will ensure they have a deep understanding of what the organization must be able to make happen.

Chapter 4

Look From the Bottom Up

Add simplicity, speed, and balance to key business processes.

The building design process does not jump from site selection to construction. A necessary interim step is the preparation of the site. When a building is to be put up, earth must be moved, waste removed, land contours altered, and a foundation laid. This preparatory activity, although not as exciting as the site selection or the actual construction, is just as vital. If it is not done properly, the building may tilt, flood, or otherwise be unusable. Similarly, organization design requires some preparatory effort to bridge the gap between grand strategy and creative structure.

After the company has been considered as a whole entity, needed functionality added, and excess functionality pruned, the work of resizing can shift gears. The skillful organization architect changes perspective from the macro to the micro.

This is the most appropriate time to apply the microscope or the magnifying glass—to conduct a close examination of the organization that is to be the vehicle for the handpicked capabilities. The object is—now, from the bottom up, from the inside out—to complete resizing by ensuring the right things are being done to convert capabilities into cash.

Eventually, as Peter Drucker is fond of observing, strategy and the big picture must degenerate into work. Resizing work has preoccupied managers throughout the world during most of the last quarter century. Getting more done with less or getting more of the right things done, or both, has been the target of countless productivity and quality improvement campaigns.

Many of these efforts have been stand-alone activities of limited impact. But those that have received senior executive championship and a multiyear commitment usually more than pay back the time and resources they consume. And those improvement campaigns that are well integrated into a companywide reexamination of strategies and structures have a real chance to make a lasting change in the ways business is conducted. In our analogy to the work of the building architect, they are the equivalent of site preparation.

What is a well-prepared site, one most ready to support the organization structure? What must happen to the activities of a company before the organization can be built around them? They need, as did the business's array of capabilities, to go through a resizing exercise.

Work has to be resized in a way that allows it to contribute three qualities to the company:

1. Simplicity
2. Speed
3. Balance

These attributes can provide focus from the bottom up, just as careful selection of capabilities and competences provides a sharp sense of top-down direction. When the tasks a company does are excessively complex, excruciatingly slow, and out of touch with the business's real needs, no amount of creative reorganizing will have much of an impact in improving the organization's performance.

Simplicity

Monroe is an American company that makes automobile shock absorbers. More than half the shock absorbers purchased in the U.S. replacement market are built by Monroe, which has also managed to crack the difficult-to-enter Japanese market. Monroe has made a great effort to improve its product quality so it could sell to Nissan and Toyota. Plant managers and engineers were sent on study tours to Japan, and what they found about management practices there surprised them. "I had always thought the Japanese were ahead because they were so automated," maintained Paul Hill, plant manager of Monroe's Hartwell, Georgia, facility. "But I realized that they were ahead because everything they set up was so simple." Work flow, plant layout, job design, mistake correction—all were designed to minimize complexity.

Hill took this lesson to heart. When he returned to Georgia, he dismantled the complicated, problem-prone factory automation system he had installed only two years before. This led to significant productivity increases—in four years Monroe-wide productivity increased by more than 25 percent—and high quality ratings from his Japanese customers. The lesson here is not that all automation is bad, but that automating the wrong ways of doings things will most likely make things worse, not better.

Businesses worldwide are realizing that there is a significant cost to complexity. Some companies, like those in Germany's *mittelstand*, avoid it by staying small, others by staying focused, like Japan's Kao. But for many, the advice of Donald Povejsil, who headed Westinghouse's corporate planning function, is closest to the mark: "One way to get significant productivity improvements is to stop unprofitable activities. When mangers stop spending all their time on insoluble problems, it's amazing how many opportunities they can find in their existing businesses."

Monroe's and Westinghouse's experiences are typical of many companies. They find that taking a hard look at what they do and how they do it is frequently more useful than many technology-based solutions. Simplicity in the workplace is an easily transferable virtue. It does not require a corporate culture rooted in Zen. It does, however, require a conscious effort at eliminating unnecessary work.

Outplacing Work—GE's Workout Process

Outplacement is a process familiar to many companies. It is a service provided to employees for whom jobs are no longer available to help them find new work. It is also an idea worth applying to surplus work. How can unneeded work be outplaced? The experience of General Electric offers some clues.

John Welch, GE's chief executive, is no stranger to criticism. Labeled "Neutron Jack" in the business press for his far-reaching organization streamlining and job cuts in the mid-1980s, he also had to face internal concerns about how work was to be done in GE's newly flattened pyramid. While many middle managers accepted intellectually the need for Welch's changes to ensure the corporation's global competitiveness, they also felt mounting pressures about doing their own jobs well.

A manager in GE's Medical Systems Group, typical of many cutback survivors, complained of excessive pressure after a layer of management was eliminated and his number of direct reports doubled from ten to twenty. "Quite honestly, I feel overworked," he lamented to a journalist. "I work hard, and sometimes I don't enjoy it anymore. . . . I don't remember a time being as busy as I am today. And it just seems like it gets busier and busier and busier." He reported instances of subordinates walking up and introducing themselves with a "Hi! Remember me? I work for you" greeting. He constantly felt he was not as available to these people as he needed to be, and he kept promising to himself: "Somehow I'm going to have to off-load some of my work."

This was a promise, Welch realized, that most middle managers were having a difficult time keeping.

There are limits to the kinds of change that can be mandated from the top of the hierarchy. Businesses can be bought and sold, as GE did, and management layers removed, but the net result may well be the conversion of the company into a corporate pressure cooker. And this pressure is something that cannot easily be released from on high, at least not without undoing many of the beneficial aspects of the restructuring. It is caused by the multitude of ways that work is done where the "rubber meets the road" and that over time become dysfunctional. Mending these ways has to start from the bottom up. But it will not necessarily start by itself.

Getting this process moving, Welch realized, was his responsibility. He structured his time so he had regular opportunities to hear middle managers "sound off," especially during his frequent appearances at GE's Crotonville, New York, management training center. He used these sessions as opportunities to engage in sharp give-and-take debates with the managers attending classes. He encouraged them to confront and to challenge the way things were commonly done. And they, in turn, tended to be open and frank about problems they were having and improvements that were needed. Welch was far enough away, hierarchically, for them to feel a degree of safety about their candor.

While sessions like these stimulated a great deal of thought, their impact had a short half-life. They basically were attempts to circumvent the hierarchy, and Welch soon realized that he needed to find a way to plug this kind of reexamination and debate into the hierarchy.

With the help of James Baughman, GE's head of executive development, a pilot program was quickly developed and launched. Welch wanted a way regularly to put all of GE's business leaders in front of from fifty to 100 of their people at a time for a no-holds-barred debate about how work was getting done. He wanted something with more staying power than the meet-the-boss, grand finale session of a typical training program.

Welch, originally from Massachusetts, patterned the sessions after the rampant democracy of New England town meetings. Like these gatherings, the GE meetings are forums for spirited debate and serious decision making. They are attended by a cross section of a business unit's work force: executives and hourly workers, middle managers and union leaders, clerks and computer professionals. And they are mandatory, not optional.

Called "workout," they are Welch's way to get rid of the "thousands of bad habits accumulated since the creation of General Electric." The name has multiple meanings. It was originally borrowed from a program to put physical fitness centers in many GE facilities, although the sessions provide more of a mental than a physical workout. It is a mechanism to work out of the organization unnecessary tasks and is done in the same tough-minded manner that bank workout specialists use when dealing with nonperforming loans.

More than a thousand workout sessions have been held throughout GE. In one year more than 40,000 employees participated in at least one of them, and the results have been impressive. A session held by NBC Sports division employees found ways to cut $1 million from the cost of televising football games. A change in production schedules in the Louisville, Kentucky, appliance factory saved over $3 million in inventory charges, and an examination of the capabilities of GE's metal workers at an aircraft engine factory in New England found the employees could redesign a part for their grinding machines better and cheaper than the outside vendor the plant management anticipated using. Appliance service technicians in Canada found a way to speed cash flow by having them write up and leave bills behind after they completed each customer call. This eliminated several steps in the invoicing process and reduced the workload of the regional office staffs.

Each unit of GE holds several workout sessions each year. The early ones tackle bothersome but relatively easy to solve issues, such as excess paperwork. Subsequent sessions deal with problems that cross organizational and turf boundaries. Teams may be made up of employees from several departments or divisions, all having a role to play on a process that cuts across organization units, like product development or order processing. After skill and comfort with the mechanics of the workout process are acquired, issues that span the company's boundaries might be considered. Suppliers and, possibly, customers may be invited to participate as equal members of workout teams. One session brought forty Sears buyers and forty GE sales-service employees together to reexamine how GE was serving Sears and jointly to plan ways to serve the buyers better.

The successful creation of workout was due in no small measure to the strong partnership formed at GE between the chief executive and the senior human resources staff. It is a program whose success depends on a blend of group dynamics and power dynamics. Senior operating executives tend to be skilled at one of these, human resources types at the other. In most companies the twain seldom meet, which explains why so many well-meaning improvement programs lead to very little real change.

Other Applications of Workout

Use of the workout process is not limited to GE. Companies as diverse as medical instrument maker Becton Dickinson, Continental Illinois Bank, and Oryx Energy have made good use of team-based work resizing. Becton Dickinson's consumer products division has organized cross-functional teams that include members from that division and other divisions, as well as suppliers and vendors. Continental set up an internal cost-cutting brigade known as Project Focus to work $40 million in expenses out of its operating budget over a two-year period. Project Focus's leader found that many of its results came from changing the way the bank did business with itself, sometimes in very simple ways: "We've tried to eliminate the redundancies, like cutting out the hard copies that used to accompany electronic mail messages." Continental's chairman, Thomas Theobald, likes to equate the bank's elimination of unnecessary meetings and related bureaucracy with a machine that has been redesigned to function with fewer moving parts.

Oryx is the world's largest independent gas and oil producer. Based in Dallas, it was spun off from Sun Oil as part of Sun's top-down refocusing in the late 1980s. Faced with a need to keep cost reductions ongoing as the price of crude oil dropped, it resized all its activities from the bottom up, with the objective of eliminating rules, reviews, reports, approvals, and other procedures that were not contributing in some way to finding hydrocarbons. Teams with representatives from all departments were organized to identify the work that did not need doing. The results were impressive. An amount equivalent to half the annual earnings was eliminated from Oryx's operating costs. An observer of the team's efforts found that "the company junked 25 percent of all internal reports, reduced from twenty to four the number of signatures required on requests for capital expenditures, and compressed from seven months to six weeks the time it took to produce the annual budget."

Outplacing work through workout is a way to rebuild simplicity into a company's workings. "For a large organization to be effective," believes John Welch, "it must be simple. For a large organization to be simple, its people must have self-confidence and intellectual self-assurance. Insecure managers create complexity. Frightened, nervous managers use thick, convoluted planning books and busy slides filled with everything they've known since childhood. People must have self-confidence to be clear, precise, to be sure that every person in their organization . . . understands what the business is trying to achieve." There is a psychological aspect to simplicity as well as an analytical one. Successful resizing requires mastery of both.

Programs such as workout can be good tools for improving productivity, but frequently the best way to resize is by adding speed.

Speed

Identifying work in need of outplacement is a little like taking a snapshot of the organization. The print can be enlarged many times to uncover duplication and lack of focus. But a snapshot captures only what is occurring at one moment in time. To get a sense of how the organization really functions, it is necessary to look at a motion picture of the sequence of events going on, not just at the still photos. Just as outplacing work is a good way to reexamine *what* a corporation is doing, a technique is also needed to consider *how* things are done.

Such a technique requires reviewing the processes used to convert raw materials to products. A *process* is a group of interrelated work activities that accomplish this sort of transformation. Processes have *cycles*, sequences of activities necessary to take something from the beginning to the end of the process. The phrase "cycle time" is used to denote how long one of these sequences takes.

In the late 1980s several management consultants "discovered" a practice already in place but relatively unnoticed—the importance of minimizing cycle time to competitive success. Two of these consultants, George Stalk and Thomas Hout, found significant financial advantages accruing to companies practicing what the companies called time compression. These companies organized their processes in ways that minimized the amount of time they required and, in doing so, sharply reduced operating expenses, improved quality, and responded fast to changes in customer needs. They were able to command prices that were from 10 to 100 percent higher than those charged by slower competitors, and their manufacturing and service costs were from 10 to 20 percent lower. They also turned over inventory several times more often than did their competition and were able to develop new products at only half the cost of their competitors' R&D efforts.

Many of the companies Stalk and Hout studied to learn about the importance of time were Japanese, but American companies such as Sun Microsystems, Wal-Mart, and Coleman, a maker of camping equipment, realized similar benefits. Coleman once had to stockpile two months of factory production just to be certain it could respond to orders from its retailer customers. After an application of time reduction techniques, it was able to make and ship an order within a week, saving $10 million because of the inventory reductions this fast cycle time allowed. Similarly, in Japan, Honda found ways to cut the time required to build motorcycles by 80 percent, and Matsushita, even more dramatically, found ways to manufacture washing machines in two hours, instead of the 360 hours previously required.

Some European businesses have also achieved significant competitive successes through speed, especially the German *mittelstand* companies. Geers, the Dortmund company that makes the miniature hearing aid favored by former President Ronald Reagan, is able to go from idea to store-displayed product in nine months. One of its key competitors, the electrical giant Siemens, required three years to move through a similar product creation and introduction cycle. Geers's time advantage is so strong that its owner claims, "We don't need patents"; time compression provides an even stronger market defense.

Like quality improvement, time-based competition has become popular in businesses throughout the world. In some cultures it has even changed executives' thought processes. Whereas business strategists used to fret about competitors winning over customers with an attractive price or cost umbrella, now the greater worry is the competition's cycle time. For others to gain an edge, they just have to do the right things quicker. For example, both General Motors and Honda announced the establishment of new car divisions at about the same time. But by the time GM's Saturn cars were arriving in dealers' showrooms, Honda's Acura had been out in the marketplace and had completed three major model changes. GM's relative slowness, or Honda's ability to operate comfortably within GM's product development cycle, is a key factor behind the market share declines of Detroit-based auto companies.

About Asian managers, one of Hout's colleagues observes: "They think about time the way we do about cost." Time is a scarce resource, something whose consumption needs to be planned and monitored. Another consultant, James Swallow, feels the most certain way to improve quality is through speed. He maintains: "Quality and cycle time are like the yin and yang. If you go after cycle time, you lower the water level in your lake, and suddenly all the rocks stick out."

What rocks? Several years ago, Toyota was dissatisfied with one of its suppliers. It was taking too long for the parts Toyota ordered to arrive. Rather than cancel the order, this being Japan, Toyota sent in some staff experts to help. They found the supplier required fifteen days to produce each component that Toyota ordered. The advisors found this could be cut to six days just by reducing the size of each order. Then they redesigned the way the supplier's factory was arranged, eliminating as many as possible of the places where inventory was building up. This took another three days off the production time. Finally all the places in the plant where partially built components were allowed to pile up were eliminated. This last improvement brought the total time from order to delivery to one day.

General Electric has also added speed by teaming with its customers. Using the workout mechanism, one GE division devised a way to let major customers enter orders directly into GE's computer system. Time saved: one week. At another division, considerable make-work time was saved when—again in the candor induced during a workout session to which customer representatives were invited—a customer admitted to throwing away without reading them six reports that GE carefully prepared for them each month!

Some Common Bottlenecks in the Time Cycle

Some of the rocks are simply unnecessary tasks. But the more dangerous shoals are the work processes that have, over time, become excessively convoluted. As with capabilities, every company has hundreds of processes. It could take years, perhaps decades, to fix all of them. Which are most worthy of having excess time wrung out? These are the three categories that have the most potential for improvement that will at the same time best enhance a company's economic value:

1. *The product development process.* All the steps that occur from idea generation to market introduction. The quicker these happen, the easier it will be to preempt competition and ensure that the customer need you are meeting is still current.
2. *The customer order process.* The activities that must occur between a customer wanting something and getting it, including those involved in making it. Speed here results both in happier customers and in lower operating costs.
3. *The problem resolution process.* Mistakes happen, things malfunction, but what can be more damaging is slowness in resolving the problems and fixing the breaks.

Some fear that concern with process speed and cycle time is a return to early twentieth-century Taylorism or to the 1950s era of stopwatch-equipped efficiency experts. But the orientation here is quite different. The idea is not so much working faster, just smarter, and enlisting the best thinking about improvements from everyone in the organization, not blindly following the advice of an outside consultant. Companies that make time awareness a key pillar of their management philosophy try to change the mind-set of their managers and employees, not just their behaviors. They instill an awareness of how interconnected everyone and every job is. And they measure the length of the connections in terms of time, not distance on an organization chart or a salary scale.

Perot Systems, a computer services company headed by the founder of Electronic Data Systems, H. Ross Perot, carries this concern with the psychological aspect of time even further. The company applies it to its reward and recognition system. When an employee accomplishes something especially significant—perhaps closing a major sale or successfully completing an extremely difficult assignment—a stock option bonus is paid that very day. There is no waiting until the end-of-the-year employee recognition banquet or merit review and no lingering period of uncertainty as the employee wonders if anyone noticed what was accomplished. But along with the immediate recognition comes a brief speech reminding the employee that the special accomplishment is now part of the company's history. "Put it behind you, and focus all of your attention on today's challenges" is the not-too-disguised message intended to be delivered by this practice.

Perhaps just-in-time bonuses can reduce some of the psychological slack that accumulates in many organizations, but dealing with organizational slack requires heavier artillery.

Reengineering Processes

"As companies grow . . . the systemlike nature of the organization often gets hidden," observes Thomas Hout, a management consultant with clients on both edges of the Pacific Rim. "Distances increase as functions focus on their own needs, support activities multiply, specialists are hired, reports replace face-to-face conversations. Before long the clear visibility of the product and the essential elements of the delivery process are lost. Instead of operating as a smoothly linked system, the company becomes a tangle of conflicting constituencies whose own demands and disagreements frustrate the customer." How can the kinks be removed from these linkages? How can the company be made whole again?

An increasingly popular way to untangle a corporation's processes and reduce its consumption of time has been dubbed "reengineering." As with the technique of workout, reengineering has political and psychological as well as technical dimensions.

From a mechanical point of view, reengineering is a way not so much to speed up the old ways of doing things but to invent new ones. It challenges the conventional wisdom and the accepted rules about how work can best be done. It tries, starting from scratch, to use break-through thinking inspired by the potential of information technologies almost literally to re-create the company. Just as workout builds on the techniques of statistical improvement, reengineering is accomplished using tools such as flow charting and work process mapping. And just as the success of workout requires the participation of those on the receiving end of the work that needs to go out, so reengineering is most likely to succeed politically and psychologically when done by a bottom-up team with a membership that cuts across the business's functions and whose efforts have top management's strong backing.

Reengineering is a frontal assault on many of the industrial practices that have shaped twentieth-century enterprise. Specialization of labor, many-step work flows, and subdivision of work into minute tasks allowed for the realization of economies of scale from the English factories of the late eighteenth and early nineteenth centuries. It also allowed them to make use of the abundant, low-skill labor that was available as many fled rural poverty. These practices were updated by Henry Ford and others a hundred years later as the factory was turned into a tool for mass production, and they were eventually imported into office settings as new work methods were needed to cope with the avalanche of paperwork that accompanied the post-World War II emergence of a mass consumer market.

These practices made increasingly less sense as the work force became better educated and more concerned with finding work that allowed the autonomy necessary to make use of the schooling. They also made less sense as mechanization allowed routine, repetitive tasks to be done by machines and robots, and information systems enabled workers to be responsible for a bigger piece of the job, without the need for close oversight from someone with "*super*-vision." But just because a practice no longer makes sense, there is no guarantee it will fade away on its own.

Except possibly at the founding of a company, seldom is much deliberate attention given to designing companywide work processes and flows. Functional competence is usually the basis for organizing most businesses (scientists in one department, accountants in another, and so on), with work passed from one functional unit to another until completed. Some reengineering practitioners like to compare this situation to the way many colonial American roads were originally laid out. The early streets followed already established cowpaths. Cows, animals that are usually in no particular hurry, tend to meander, as did many of these dirt roads. When the time came to "improve" (pave) the roads, their routings were already well taken for granted, and they were simply paved over. Decades later, the advent of the motorcar made speed more of a possibility and straight roads more of a necessity. Straightening the cowpaths, though, is usually far from straightforward. In the intervening years, many structures have been built along the twisting paths, and the paving tended to give an aura of permanence to the original route.

Balance

Speed and simplicity are important attributes of the new corporation. But these qualities need to be pursued with both eyes open. Sometimes it makes sense to add costs. For example, job cuts among the fish cleaning crews at H. J. Heinz's StarKist tuna canning factories so overworked those remaining that literally tons of meat were left on the fish bones each day. Staffing was then increased, the extra payroll costs more than covered by the extra production.

Heinz also found that sometimes it is worthwhile to slow the production line. Sales of its formerly popular potato product, Tater Tots, were declining. Consumers had noticed that its once chunky taste had turned mushy. The cause: new high-speed potato-cutting machines. The machines were slowed down, and the chunky taste returned, as did the customers. The sales increase easily covered the cost of the process slowdown.

Citicorp once received many favorable comments in the business press for its fast home mortgage approval process. In the mid-1980s, it set out to become the dominant U.S. housing lender, using this speedy process to provide loans to buyers who provided little or no information about their income or assets. After several years and a lingering recession, the strategy backfired, and repayment of many billions of dollars of its loan portfolio was significantly overdue.

The view from the bottom up needs to be balanced with that from the top down. Mutual Benefit Life did all the "right" things in making microimprovements to its insurance application process. But these did not prevent strategic miscalculations that forced the New Jersey state insurance regulators to seize the company and take top management control away from a creative process reengineer. Instead, turnaround artist Victor Palmieri was put in charge of rehabilitating the insurer from the top down.

The resizing issue is really one of design: How should work and work processes best be configured? While it is impossible to provide one answer suitable for everything that goes on in a complex organization, the parallels between physical and organization design provide some clues.

It is very difficult to specify what makes a good design good. It is part a matter of aesthetics, part a matter of personal preference. But over time, design professionals and their critics have tended to favor simplicity over clutter, economy over extravagance, and a sense of proportion over exaggeration. Too much of a good thing, whether it be management practice or artistic flourish, can be dangerous.

Tools are available to help find the right degree of balance. Applying judgment and logic is usually helpful, and sometimes analogies can guide the logic. Analogies can also suggest some new ways to think about old problems. For example, here is a way to reconsider the evils of overhead expenses.

Cholesterol and Overhead

Overhead is a lot like cholesterol. Both have been targets of severe criticism. Both can induce fatty deposits; one clogs the insides of human arteries, the other congests a corporation's metabolism.

Both have been severely misunderstood. Cholesterol plays a very important role in human chemistry. It forms the nucleus of the vitamin D molecule, the nutrient that builds strong bones. It is a component of several sex and regulatory hormones and contributes to the fluidity of cell membranes. Often thought to be fat, it isn't. Actually it helps make the bile salts that emulsify fats in the intestine.

Cholesterol is manufactured within the body. Problems arise, though, when it is ingested. Its internal production goes on regardless of the amount taken in, and its chemistry is such that it is hard to break down once a surplus occurs.

Cholesterol comes in two types, depending on how it is being transported in the bloodstream. As those who have had tests for cholesterol know, one of these types (called "HDL") is sometimes dubbed "good cholesterol" because it moves to the liver where it can do something useful for the body. "Bad cholesterol" (identified as "LDL") tends to stay put, thus resulting in deposits on artery walls. Heart attacks are often associated with high levels of the LDL variety, and decreased risk of having coronary disease with concentrations of HDL.

The relative balance between HDL and LDL is, in part, controllable. LDL increases when diets are rich in animal fats; regular aerobic exercise leads to more HDL.

Overhead, like cholesterol, is something that naturally occurs to make effective functioning possible. It plays a key role in regulating the proper balance among a business's diverse activities. As with cholesterol, problems arise when too much overhead is imposed on the business from the outside. It is hard to remove once in place and, like some people's dietary limitation regimes, it can be painful to cut back. Corporate aerobics, such as workout, can keep overhead in check, but only temporarily.

There are also two kinds of overhead: good and bad. Good carries its own weight, and then some; bad only contributes bulk. The processes considered earlier, workout and process reengineering, are good tools to help make these distinctions. But in some cases, a deeper, more thoughtful, examination is necessary than can be provided in the gung-ho, take-no-prisoners atmosphere of these outplacement mechanisms for work and time.

Good and Bad Overhead

Contrast the ways strategic planning has been carried out in two major businesses: the LTV Corporation and Royal Dutch Shell. Dallas-based LTV was, by the late 1960s, a prototypical complex conglomerate. Operating in a variety of businesses, including aerospace, shipbuilding, and steel, it needed a number of mechanisms to keep central control over the diversity. A key mechanism was its planning process.

Developed by a large consulting firm, Booz, Allen, & Hamilton, and ingested into LTV, this system in the mid-1970s required each division to prepare and send to Dallas a two-inch-thick planning study each year. The head of LTV's steel unit at that time was Thomas Graham, an irreverent, combative enemy of corporate bureaucracy. He was convinced the planning documents were having little impact on how the company was operating, other than via the consumption of the resources required to generate them. He even suspected the LTV headquarters staff was not bothering to read them, so he tried an experiment.

One year, at plan submission time, he put a new cover sheet on the previous year's study and sent it on. Not receiving any comment on this "updated" plan, he became bolder. The next year's submission also was that of two years earlier, with an updated cover and several sections in the report's middle whited out. Again, no sign his mischief was detected: "No one ever said a word," Graham maintains.

Strategic planning at Royal Dutch Shell has engaged the talents of senior executives in a less delinquent fashion. Shell is a world leader in the development and use of scenario-based planning. "Scenario" is a theatrical term that has entered both the military and the business vocabularies. It refers to the script and directions actors in a play or film are expected to follow. When used in corporate planning, scenarios tend to be stories, part fact and part conjecture, intended to stimulate thinking about the future. They are not forecasts per se, but possibilities—illustrations of how things might turn out.

Shell was one of the few companies to have anticipated—and thought out contingency plans to cope with—both the unexpected sharp price increases instituted by the Organization of Petroleum Exporting Countries (OPEC) in the 1970s and the surprise free-fall in oil prices a decade later. This occurred not because Shell had a clearer crystal ball than other companies, but as a result of its ongoing use of scenarios that dealt with a wide range of possible oil prices. The scenarios were researched and written by a talented team of in-house futurists. This team traveled throughout the Shell network of offices, presenting these alternative futures to executives in ways that engaged their imaginations, stimulated their thinking, and encouraged them to consider and prepare for far-out possibilities. These discussions, in turn, helped identify the decisions Shell executives would need to make, depending on which ways oil prices actually moved.

LTV and Shell represent two ways to go about long-range planning. One involves filling out forms, the other rehearsing the future. In one, the information produced by the planning process enters a black hole at headquarters; in the other, the central staff leave their offices and creatively stimulate the thinking of the rest of the company. One is a worthy candidate for work outplacement, the other an important contributor to balance between the future and the present. One plays the role of LDL in its corporation's metabolism; the other acts more like HDL. Both processes are costly in terms of staff salaries and management time. Across-the-board cutbacks in both companies would be counterproductive. In one, needed muscle would be harmed; in the other, the cuts would probably not go deep enough.

When resizing, overhead quality can be more important than quantity. Time-compression guru Thomas Hout observed a Michigan auto parts maker whose overhead was twice as large as that of its Japanese affiliate. But the real difference was not so much the size of the overhead as the type. Even though the Japanese manufacturer had only half the administrative head count, twice as many of the administrators held jobs whose purpose was to make things better in the company by improving processes—jobs such as R&D engineers, materials managers, purchasing coordinators, and process development specialists. They were "good overhead" (process improvers), focused on the company's future. At the

Figure 6. The resizing process.

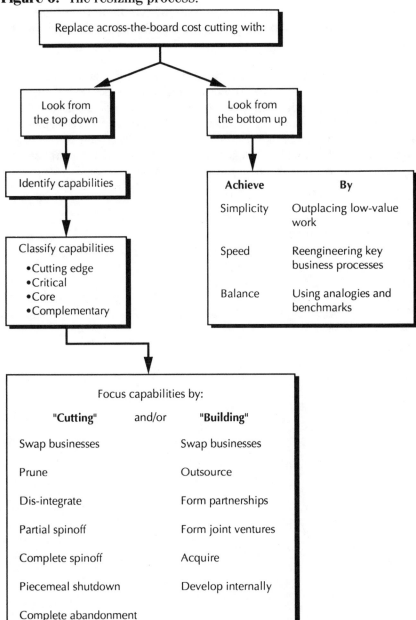

Michigan company, on the other hand, the more "today"-oriented over-head jobs, such as expediters, extra material handlers, inspectors, and miscellaneous troubleshooters, outnumbered the Japanese improvers by four to one.

The resizing techniques described in this chapter and in Chapter 3 are summarized in Figure 6. They may seem to be like taking the long way around to building the new corporation. But tools like capability analysis, outplacement of unnecessary work, and process reengineering are essential to prepare its foundation. Too many reorganizations impatiently start with lines and boxes, centralization and decentralization, jobs and head count. And many of these also fail.

PART TWO
RESHAPE

Chapter 5

Repeal the Industrial Revolution

Avoid the toxic side effects of work fragmentation.

Thinking about reshaping a company usually starts by considering the attributes of its organizational structure. How tall or flat, pyramidal or rectangular is it? Is its orientation inward toward its operating procedures or outward toward its customers? Is it tightly centralized or a collection of semiautonomous fiefdoms?

These are important concerns, but they are not the first issues that need to be addressed. Decisions about *what* is being structured need to come first. What is the nature of the boxes that the lines are to connect? Are we using structure to organize people, jobs, departments, or something else? Just what should be the basic building blocks of the corporation? What are their most needed characteristics, and how must they function in an era of turbulence and change?

Unfortunately, these questions seldom receive close attention during organization restructuring. *What is being structured* is frequently taken for granted. Where the lines go on an organization chart usually gets more attention than what the boxes consist of. Too often, debate about structural type clouds consideration of how much *the choice of structure depends on what that structure is made from.*

This chapter and Chapter 6 explore the problems with, and the alternatives to, the organizational building blocks commonly in use. Chapters 7 and 8 then consider the kinds of fast, nonbureaucratic structures possible to design from these alternative building blocks.

Organizational Building Blocks

Companies frequently give lip service to "people" as the basic unit around which the company is organized. Unfortunately this emphasis on people tends to be more of an aspiration than an accomplishment. Employees are frequently given token acknowledgement as the business's "most important asset," but their characteristics are then felt to vary too much or to be too unstable to serve as the real basis around which most corporate organizations can be planned.

Reconfiguring each individual's psychological makeup or each member's wants and needs to accommodate the organization's requirements, would be similar to an architect's attempting to reengineer the molecules that comprised the steel or concrete to be used in a building. It is not an impossible task and may lead to some useful innovations, but the skill required is beyond that possessed by the architect. Likewise, the organization planner is usually unable to adjust motivations and personalities to the requirements of the organization (not that some have not tried!) but must ensure the organization design realistically reflects individual potentials and limitations.

Unfortunately few organizations deal well with individual needs. Instead, contemporary organizations tend to be built from the pairing of "workers and bosses." What the company needs to have done is usually thought of functionally: Design something, make it, sell it, service it. The functions are subdivided by skill level, and individual jobs are then defined around the resulting subdivisions. Integral to the job being accomplished, but apart from the work of the accomplisher, is the overseer or boss.

A Legacy of the Industrial Revolution

Organizing along functional lines may have made good sense at the start of the Industrial Revolution, as thousands of unskilled farm laborers came to work in the early factories. It even had some appropriateness in the mid-twentieth century as industries across the world joined a mass production race to satisfy decades of pent-up consumer demand resulting from World War II and the Great Depression. But today, the practices of functionally dividing labor and of separating the supervisor from what is being supervised have become outmoded and counterproductive.

Some of the difficulties with the functional division of labor were apparent from the outset. Adam Smith, the economist usually credited with giving the Industrial Revolution its intellectual justification, also provided a frequently ignored warning in *The Wealth of Nations:* "The man whose whole life is spent performing a few simple operations has no occasion to exert his understanding. . . . He naturally loses, therefore, the habit of such exertion, and generally becomes as stupid and ignorant as it is possible for a human creature to become."

Concerns such as these have set the agenda for many political philosophers and social scientists ever since. Karl Marx elaborated on the downside of the Industrial Revolution in many of his writings; Emile Durkheim, considered the father of modern sociology, took the opposite tack and stressed the need for workers to get help adjusting to the new realities of industrial life. These arguments continued for many decades, with many humanistically oriented psychologists decrying the alienation of the workers, and others, taking minute division of labor as a modern economic necessity, suggesting ways to ameliorate its worst consequences. Frederick Taylor was one such rational reformer, Elton Mayo, of Hawthorne experiment fame, another. A generation later, organization development experts took cues from Chris Argyris and his critique of many industrial environments as places poor at furthering psychological growth and self-esteem.

From these efforts have come many prescriptions for improvement. Experiments in workplace democracy, employee involvement, and empowerment have been tried in many companies, but their track record is mixed. Some have had positive results, such as those put in place by Ford and by Procter and Gamble in the 1980s. Some have failed and been discarded. Others have been valiant efforts with only limited results, like the attempt at Volvo to dismantle the assembly line in a new plant in Uddevalla, Sweden.

In Uddevalla, some Volvo watchers felt the company was trying to turn its back on the Industrial Revolution. There, a factory was designed to enable a small team of highly skilled workers to assemble an entire car. During this two- to three-hour process, the team is aided by a state-of-the-art system for materials handling that allows team members to keep their attention on just the task at hand. Each eight-to-ten-employee team works on several cars at once, and each team member receives enough training to be able to do at least half the jobs required to assemble a Volvo.

Unfortunately, the total number of labor hours to build a car this way is more than twice those required to produce the same result in Volvo's more traditional assembly line plant in Belgium and almost three times as many as are spent by its heavily automated Japanese competitors.

Lest the baby disappear with the dirty bathwater, Volvo's experiment at least had a measure of success in dealing with some of the human problems of the traditional assembly line: worker boredom leading to excessive absenteeism and turnover. But for solutions to be lasting, they must address economic as well as humanistic concerns. After several profitless years, Volvo announced the Uddevalla plant's closing.

Volvo was probably on the right track, though. Perhaps returning, conceptually at least, to the Middle Ages might be a useful way to see where things went wrong when the world industrialized.

The Skill Hierarchy Before Adam Smith

While most economic activity in pre-Industrial Revolution Europe centered around agriculture and trading, a formal system of guilds existed for several hundred years to guide the development of skill- and knowledge-based products. Though some existed mainly to enforce their monopoly over a particular craft or technique, most guilds also ensured that a mechanism was in place for new entrants to the field, called apprentices, to learn the trade. Apprentices started by developing speed and accuracy and learning good work habits. After a several-year training period, under the direction of an established "master," they were certified as journeymen able to practice their craft wherever they could find work.

At times, journeymen worked with several established masters to get exposure to as many aspects of their craft as possible. Journeymen stonemasons, for example, often used this period of their careers to visit nearby cathedrals to study their construction, and to add new building techniques to their repertoire. In addition to rounding out the individual journeymen's skill base, these exposures to different approaches and customer requirements helped diffuse know-how among practitioners of the craft.

This method of supervised and self-directed experience gathering ensured that every skill necessary to produce whatever the journeyman made was part of his repertoire (almost all were men at the time these practices developed). The seasoned artisan of the Middle Ages actually had two classes of skill. One was in-depth knowledge of the various routines and subroutines required by his particular craft—carpentry, jewelry making, boatbuilding, or whatever. The other was the flexibility necessary to know when to shift from one routine to another as the customer-specific requirements for his end product dictated. Each journeyman had to do many particular things well.

The master was at the top of the craft hierarchy. He also had acquired several other types of skills, probably by imitating the actions of more successful and established masters. One skill was the inventiveness needed to advance the overall development of the craft. Another was the teaching ability necessary to develop apprentices. A third was the merchant instincts required to sell what he had made. Staying close to the customer was built into the master artisan's job description—the factory was frequently also the store.

This way of organizing work tended to produce small enterprises, structured more like a diamond than a pyramid. Often set up as family workshops, they were based in the master's home, with support services provided by members of the master's family. Each master employed two or three journeymen and one or two apprentices.

Not all operations were so small. A variant on this pattern, useful when the market for the artisan's product was large and the cost of raw materials high, was an interconnected network of small workshops. The work of these shops was coordinated by a merchant entrepreneur with access to some capital, who advanced raw material, saw that production was coordinated when it involved several workshops working sequentially, and then sold or exported the production. These early enterprises were common throughout Europe. And they were not all what we think of as small cottage industries: a massive 60,000-person textile-producting network was centered in Florence in the mid-1300s, and a similarly large and thriving fifteenth-century metalworking group was based near Cologne.

The Era of Fragmentation

Then came the Industrial Revolution. Driven by a combination of capital-intensive new technologies, newly emerged mass markets, and global trade based on national competitive advantage, production was organized around the idea of division of labor instead of craft specialization. The work formerly done by one artisan was broken down into its component parts, which in turn were mechanized where possible, and semi-skilled workers were hired to do part of the job or to tend the machines. New roles, those of supervisor, middle manager, and production planner, were created to provide the oversight and coordination that were formerly the responsibility of individual journeymen or masters. In brief, *authority over the content of jobs was given to people who, themselves, were not actually doing the work.* This newly created managerial authority took "from workers the right to define their own job, their own skill level, their own standards of quality."

The division of labor, originally intended to create a rapid growth economy based on a low-skill work force, did help assimilate nineteenth-century agricultural workers into industry. But once there, it imprisoned them.

Division of labor is an addictive practice. Work breakdown—promoted by those whose authority and careers tend to benefit from it—tends to beget more work breakdown, taking the pressure off the employer or the educational system to continually upgrade employee skills. Once started, the practice tends to be self-reinforcing, producing a de-skilled work force. One American executive echoed Adam Smith during mass production's heyday in the 1950s: "One has the feeling of division of labor having gone wild, far beyond any degree necessary for efficient production." He called this practice "fantastically wasteful" for both industry and society because it does not make use of people's "complex and multiple capacities."

By the mid-twentieth century, most corporate organizations were based on the concept of functional specialization. Work that was once whole had become fragmented. The focused skill of an individual was diffused into the skill of an entire factory. And, in the words of one shipbuilder working in a twentieth-century shipyard organized around this logic: "The common view was that mechanics check their brains at the gate when they come to work."

Bucking the Trend: More Lessons From the *Mittelstand*

This shipbuilder's lament is true for many—but not all—corporations. Excessive division of labor is a problem many of Germany's *mittelstand* companies have managed to escape. They take advantage of a strong national apprenticeship program to ensure their incoming workers are well-grounded in the skills most critical to competitiveness. As mentioned in Chapter 3, they keep their business focused around a few key capabilities, so they can afford to remain state-of-the-art in them. Few medieval goldsmiths attempted to grow revenues by also doing some blacksmithing or stone carving on the side.

Just as the master artisan had regular contact with his customers, many *mittelstand* companies avoid isolating employees with customer contact responsibilities into sales or service departments. When customers call with problems, a team with members both from the factory and from the product development lab may be dispatched, along with the customer service technician. In addition to all contributing to the problem's solution, all carry back to their ongoing assignments a greater appreciation for what happens when their company's product leaves the safety of the factory walls. The chief executives of these companies also spend a high percentage of their time away from headquarters and with customers. Ideas for product enhancements frequently come from these visits, and more than once the company president has been forced to rely on his detailed product knowledge to perform an on-the-spot repair.

When in-person customer contact is difficult—as is the situation at Claas, a *mittelstand* builder of harvesting machines that sells primarily through independent farm equipment distributors—innovation replaces organizational rigidity. Claas set up several company-run retail outlets, not to compete with their distributors but to create a forum for direct customer contact. Employees from a variety of Claas's functional units spend time in these stores, interacting with farmers and keeping abreast of their harvesting needs. This keeps Claas from relying solely on the filtered information that distributors or third-party market researchers might provide.

While these German companies have never lost their link to the era of guilds and master artisans, some other industries are taking advantage of new technologies to recover some of the "wholeness" that once characterized most jobs. The American steel industry is one that is moving full circle on this issue.

The 1890s were a time of great turmoil in the steel industry. New steelmaking technologies, coupled with strongly increasing demand for relatively uniform products, led industry executives to reconsider the craftlike organization of jobs in the steel mills. The labor conflicts that arose from this reorganization led to many violent work stoppages, but the industry eventually structured the jobs in a way that put a management group more in control of the production process. Then started an industrial roller coaster: many decades of compounded growth and prosperity, followed by an abrupt decline.

Currently, this industry, in a much weaker position as the market for steel has globalized, is using modern minimill technology to rebuild its competitiveness. One of the leading minimill producers, Texas-based Chaparral Steel, has become the world's lowest-cost steelmaker, in part, by eliminating the now dysfunctional organizational principles of the Industrial Revolution. Distinctions between workers and managers are difficult to find. All dress the same, are paid salaries, and drink the same company-provided coffee. All are expected to keep customers happy and to keep the technology current. All are part of a continuing education program that stresses the core technical and business disciplines Chaparral's operations are based on. New mills are built with heavy employee input into their design; recently two maintenance workers invented a $60,000 machine that tied bundles of steel rods together and that replaced a slower $250,000 device.

This company, like many of the *mittelstand* businesses, minimizes the functional split between those who make and those who sell. Every one of its 900 employees is required to make sales calls.

Efforts such as these to combat the toxic effects of the Industrial Revolution need to fight fragmentation of work and jobs. Eliminating excessive work fragmentation requires rethinking the way work has been packaged into jobs, or, in other words, *reconsidering the nature of the basic building blocks of our companies.*

Too often, the *individual worker* and the *worker's boss* are assumed to be these basic building blocks. As the primary "raw materials" from which the company's structure is fashioned, these "building blocks" need to be examined closely to ensure they can respond adequately to the wide range of pressures facing the new corporation. While companies preparing for the twenty-first century cannot mechanistically revert to the Middle Ages to find organization structures to imitate, they can adapt that period's concept of job wholeness to create new ways to get work done in the post-Industrial Revolution era.

Here is where reference to the logic of architecture may be helpful. Building architects, more than most organization designers, are carefully taught not to ignore the properties of the materials they are considering when planning a new design. Serious mistakes in the choice of construction material can result in either collapse with the first strong wind or bankruptcy of the building's owner as he struggles to cover the costs of an overbuilt building. Let's look closely at how these choices are made in architecture to seek parallels to help guide this too frequently glossed-over aspect of organization design.

A Structure's Shape Is Constrained by the Materials It Is Made From

What are the initial choices an architect must make when starting to design a building? After consideration has been given to the site and its preparation, the designer selects an appropriate building material. Will the structure be made of stone or brick, wood or glass, concrete or steel, or some combination of these? These decisions come early in the structural design process because the characteristics of the material chosen, to a great extent, determine the kinds of structures possible to build.

During Greece's Golden Age, builders were acutely aware of the limitations of stone. The size of their door and window openings was limited to about ten feet, the size of the stone that could bridge two columns without breaking in the center and crashing. To get around this restriction, the Romans invented concrete, enabling them to construct massive aqueducts and the famous Colosseum. But finding an alternative to the "heavy look" and the large sites required by these concrete and stone structures had to wait almost 2,000 years until engineers such as Gustave Eiffel and John Roebling perfected the use of structural steel. Today, combinations of concrete and steel make commonplace spans many times wider and taller than those found in classical structures.

How Materials Help Structures Deal With Change

Good construction materials need more than raw strength to be useful. Strength is fine when coping with the day-to-day forces a building must endure: its own weight and that of its occupants. But at times the pressures on a building are less predictable and more extreme—hurricane-force winds, an overcapacity crowd, mountains of snow deposited by a once-in-a-century blizzard, or the motion trauma induced by an unexpected earthquake.

Most materials change shape when under pressure. The quality of a material that allows dynamic forces to be managed and enables the material to return to its original appearance when the pressure stops is called *elasticity*. Most materials, within limits, are elastic. But when these limits are exceeded, the material becomes permanently deformed. Such a material is then said to behave *plastically*.

There are limits to plasticity. If the pressures continue, materials eventually fail and the structures they support crumble. This is what happened to the Oakland Bay Bridge during the 1989 California earthquake. Other, less sudden, but equally devastating changes in plasticity have led to the collapses of one of the great Egyptian pyramids in Meidum and of a beautiful but never finished Gothic cathedral north of Paris in Beauvais.

Some materials, such as glass, do not provide the observable warning of plastic deformation before they fail. Their inherent *brittleness* makes them useless in situations where the forces on them can quickly come and go. This is why glass, which actually is stronger than steel in dealing with forces such as tension and compression, is useless for most structural purposes.

Of course, architects also consider nonstructural factors when choosing materials with which to build. Cost is always a consideration, as is availability. The inherent beauty of a material and how well it harmonizes with the site and its surroundings are seldom ignored. But it is the structural properties—strength, elasticity, plasticity, and brittleness—that most frequently veto the choice of building block.

Selecting Appropriate Materials

To cope with the limitations inherent in building materials, architects use a number of strategies when selecting basic building blocks:

- *They look for materials, such as concrete, that can be reinforced.* Combining two materials in one building block allows them to complement each other and gives that block greater strength and versatility.

- *They consider composites when possible.* Composites are a mixture of several materials. Unlike a reinforced substance, in which each material retains its own identity and properties, a composite is a new material with unique characteristics. Concrete was an early composite, made by combining cement with sand, stone pebbles, and water. Some plastics have properties that may make them attractive composite ingredients in future composite materials. Making a composite frequently requires the expenditure of energy and careful watch over the proportions of each ingredient.

- *They differentiate load- from non-load-bearing materials.* They make sure that only materials with appropriate structural qualities are used in situations where they must support the building. Materials whose contribution is primarily aesthetic are not ignored; they are just kept away from these places.

Architects never take the characteristics of their building materials too much for granted. They cannot. The structural integrity of their work depends on their choice of building blocks and their knowledge of how the blocks cope with change. Organization designers must be equally as careful as they specify corporate building blocks with sufficient mettle to resist the pressures generated by a globalizing economy.

Corporate Structure in the Global Economy

A wide range of forces has become a constant part of the business landscape. One is the pressure to get more done for less, a "push" in some ways similar to the compressive force on materials used in building construction. As the world's economies become less local, more interconnected, the globalizing labor market will work to the severe disadvantage of any business with less than world-class productivity. This reality will result in an ongoing requirement, for many companies, to maximize resources, to squeeze more out of what they have. This is not a pressure that will come and go with fluctuations of the business cycle but an ongoing fact of life during the next several decades as an integrated global economy emerges.

Corporate structures will be increasingly expected to deal with tension-producing forces, as well as compressive ones. Among them is the tendency for companies to become increasingly spread thin as they respond to an expanding multitude of masters. If the 1980s was a decade when shareholders demanded special attention, the 1990s have started with the customers' wishes being placed on a pedestal. And before the decade closes it is likely that both employees and their governments will take their turn demanding greater attention to their particular needs and requirements. On top of these whiplash-inducing pressures will be the ongoing operational tensions arising from the continuing use of speed as a competitive weapon.

As if these ongoing pushes and pulls will not be enough of a challenge, most businesses will also face the requirement to be more flexible than ever in deploying and redeploying resources to match the moving targets provided by customers' requirements and competitors' advances. The globalizing marketplace tends to be unforgiving when corporate inertia or bureaucracy limits flexibility. This degree of organizational elasticity—stretching to accommodate special situations, then returning to the original shape to meet regular demands—is already a necessity in many industries. Soon it will be mandatory in most.

A measure of plasticity will be needed, as well. The ability to change an organization's shape, to adapt to new markets or to reconfigure around emerging capabilities, will be another dynamic quality in the repertoire of the new corporation. This attribute—the ability to reorganize completely every several years without succumbing to terminal brittleness—is a rarity in most companies today. But it will be common among those that thrive into the coming century.

What material is best at handling this combination of static and dynamic forces? How should a company package its jobs to have the strength to deal with tension and compression? How can the qualities of elasticity and plasticity be maximized and that of brittleness avoided?

Just as architects have never found a single, always appropriate building block for every structure, organization designers are also unlikely to find one. But the old building blocks of narrowly defined jobs used in tandem with traditional supervision are not working. Perhaps the lead of the architect can be followed, and companies can learn to select organizational building blocks that can be adjusted to cope with the forces they face at a particular time. In keeping with what has worked for the architect, organization planners can:

▪ Reinforce jobs to ensure they have the strength to resist the tensions and compressions they must increasingly cope with.

▪ Use the organizational equivalent of composites—teams—when job reinforcement alone is insufficient to provide the company with an appropriate degree of flexibility.

▪ Make sure that the company's managers are in load-bearing roles—ones vital to the organization's structural integrity—and act as drivers of the business's ongoing adaptability, rather than mere definers of unneeded internal walls.

Reinforced jobs, composite teams, and load-bearing managers— these may well be the most useful raw materials from which the structure of the new corporation is shaped. Chapter 6 examines how each differs from the building blocks currently in place in most businesses.

Chapter 6
Make Work Whole Again

Reinforce jobs, build strong teams, and make middle managers load-bearing.

Companies that are structured to eliminate the self-inflicted wound of job fragmentation have three types of positions. Some employees are solo contributors, but their jobs are reinforced, not unnecessarily constricted. Others serve as full-time team members. They are responsible for adding to their group's effort so the team regularly produces results beyond those reasonable to expect from the same number of individual performers. A relatively small number of employees are designated managers. They are in load-bearing roles, rather than in part-time-manager-part-time-worker jobs. They set direction and monitor results for the individual and team efforts, but they are not in a social caste apart from everyone else.

Let's look at the attributes of these three types of positions, starting with what is required to reinforce a job.

Reinforced Jobs

How can a job be reinforced? Concrete is reinforced by pouring it over well-placed steel bars. What kinds of "steel" are worth adding to jobs as they are being designed? Three functional equivalents to steel bars are worth considering as built-in reinforcements for most positions. They are *depth*, *flex*, and *self-control*.

Depth

A job can acquire strength, or *depth*, by having a good measure of substance or content to it. In most cases, this means structuring assignments so brains are required as well as brawn. John Welch probably said it best in a section of GE's annual report on work redesign efforts: "People who had never been asked for anything other than their time and their hands now saw their minds, their views sought after."

Kodak has moved in this direction in its precision components division. For many years, Daniel Cardinale, an assembly worker there, did little but operate his punch press machine. Now, in addition to meeting his production responsibilities, he is expected to coach less senior employees in statistical process control, meet frequently with representatives from the companies that supply the raw materials he works with, and help select new employees. He repairs his machine when it breaks, monitors his own productivity, and is expected to contribute to the success of a just-in-time inventory program, rather than just being a cog in its wheel. Beefing up jobs along these lines has had a clear economic payoff for Kodak: Cardinale's work group produces almost three times the amount of work it did when jobs were more narrowly designed.

IBM has created more depth in its Austin, Texas, assembly line jobs by training many blue-collar workers to measure the speed and accuracy of their production processes and to test the quality of the products they produce. The result was a significant increase in the productivity of the engineering professionals who formerly did this work, in addition to meeting their product and process design responsibilities. The leverage provided by the retrained assembly workers allowed the engineers to acquire more depth in the work for which they added the greatest value.

This principle of leveraging senior talent with that of juniors is seriously underexploited in most companies, even though its payback can be great. Research reveals that, often, significant portions—frequently 50 to 75 percent—of the work time of expensive technical talent and key sales producers is spent on activities that they do not personally need to do. This detracts from their ability to provide the greatest value to their employers. Over time, this pattern leads to overstaffing with senior talent and underutilizing those in more junior ranks. This waste of talent is especially apparent when researchers compare the content of American engineers' jobs with that of their Japanese counterparts. According to one Arthur D. Little study, the typical Japanese engineer spends two to three times as many hours in each workday doing actual engineering as does his or her counterpart across the Pacific.

The economic importance of leveraging skills—adding depth to more junior jobs—is underscored by a study conducted by a former Xerox executive, Paul Strassmann, of staffing levels and financial performance in 292 major companies. He found the businesses with the highest profitability tended to be those with the most clerks or support staff per knowledge worker. This finding calls into question the knee-jerk reaction of many companies when they begin cost cutting: first eliminating these support positions.

Obtaining leverage through technology enabled Saab-Scania, Sweden's second-largest automaker, to avoid some of the diseconomies that plagued Volvo. In Trollhattan, a town only a few miles from Volvo's innovative Uddevalla plant, Saab built a large factory heavily staffed with fully functioning robots.

Rather than following Volvo's tack of humanizing the car assembly job, Saab found ways to take humans out of the process—at least out of the direct part assembly job. The doer job at Trollhattan is to run the robots, repair them when needed, and make decisions about replacing them after so many breakdowns. By reconceptualizing a higher-order role for workers, Saab added depth to these highly trained technician positions, rather than following the Volvo attempt to reverse the flow of industrialization.

Many jobs, including those in service industries, can provide economic benefits if they are reinforced. The successful reengineering of the insurance application approval process at Mutual Benefit Life heavily depended on creation of a new customer service job that did tasks formerly handled by nineteen employees scattered across the company. In the early 1990s, the Coca-Cola Company surveyed the chief executives of the largest U.S. food retailers. They were asked to think about ways that the jobs of customer contact employees in supermarkets—primarily stock clerks and cashiers—could be changed to contribute to increased store revenues. More than three-quarters of these numbers-driven executives felt that they would get significant sales increases if they did three things:

1. Provided clerks with information about the products the store sold, especially regarding nutritional value and methods of preparation.
2. Gave these employees basic training in suggestive or consultative selling.
3. Taught them ways to obtain and remember customers' names (retailing research found that calling a customer by name does a great deal to ensure repeat visits to the store).

All three of these job reinforcements significantly reposition the store clerk's role. No longer just a cog in a company's food distribution chain, clerks are now expected to use more of their latent talent to advance the company's broader merchandising mission.

The quality of depth has been successfully added to a job when each worker can see the beginning and the end of the major tasks on which the most time is spent. The shelf stocker's job does not end—or pay off for the retailer—when the goods are placed on the shelf. They have to end up in the customer's hand. The position is strengthened by adding both new skills and broader access to information. Jobs reinforced this way allow for a modern equivalent of the career progression from apprentice to master—something not possible if most of a person's effort goes toward just fastening a bolt, entering data on a computer terminal, or watching for a light to go on on a machine's control panel.

Flex

Strength can also be added by building *flex*—multifunctionality—into the way jobs are designed. Closely related to a job's depth, flex allows one individual, through extensive cross-training, routinely to perform more than one job. Flex is the key to the high productivity and customer responsiveness of companies such as RailTex, an operator of many small feeder railroad lines scattered from California to Virginia. Most of these were unprofitable branches of larger railroads that RailTex took over. Unlike workers in the narrowly defined job descriptions common to most unionized carriers, RailTex's employees are expected to perform a variety of roles. When a locomotive engineer has some slack time after finishing switching cars for a customer's delivery, he may wash the locomotive, handle the paperwork necessary for billing, or make a few sales calls on other nearby customers.

The women's fashion chain The Limited has prospered in a time of bankruptcy-inducing sales declines for many retailers by following a strategy of focus and flexibility. A large shopping mall may include several of its stores, including The Limited, Limited Express, Victoria's Secret, and Cacique. Each store has a very distinct look and merchandising mix from the customer's viewpoint, but the stockrooms at the back of the stores are interconnected with passageways and stairs to allow sales attendants to move from store to store as customer traffic dictates. This arrangement also allows for a single "mall manager" to replace several individual store heads, as well as for a smaller total work force than would be required by several stand-alone operations. Realizing these benefits requires more than behind-the-scenes architectural changes. All clerks and managers have to be trained to be knowledgeable about each store's merchandise and customer preferences. And all must have mastered the skill of rapidly shifting gears.

In another service industry—upscale hotels—the Oriental chain has gained considerable distinction for personalized, on-demand service, thanks to an extensive cross-training effort. If you happen to be a luncheon speaker at a rival hotel—say, a Hilton, Hyatt, or Marriott—a request for help setting up your slide projector will most likely be met with a polite "Certainly. Please wait a minute and I'll page someone from our audiovisual department to come here and help you." No such wait is needed, though, at the San Francisco Oriental. Ask any waiter or busboy for such assistance, and he will stop whatever he is doing and immediately make the projector function to your satisfaction. All customer contact employees have been trained to handle personally most requests guests might make.

Manufacturing companies are also discovering many benefits from having a cross-trained factory work force. Both General Motors and Toyota have found teamwork and quality improvement efforts thrive when employees have more than a passing understanding of the work done by their colleagues. At a General Motors plant, cross-training the workers who assembled automobile suspension systems resulted in almost eliminating the warranty costs incurred when defective systems were sold and had to be repaired. This happened because workers at each stage of the production process had become sufficiently knowledgeable about what should have happened previously to be able to spot—and fix—defects before they became buried within the assembled car.

Problem avoidance is an important benefit of investing in flex. Another advantage, which brings with it the side benefit of helping lower hierarchal walls, is illustrated by the unique approach taken by the Vanguard Group to coping with sharp upward surges in workload. Most of this mutual fund distributor's customer contact is by telephone. Orders to buy or sell shares or to transfer money from one mutual fund to another are handled by a well-trained and well-organized group of telephone representatives. The size of this operation is adequate to handle the normal peaks and valleys of inquiries and trading. But special events—stock market crashes or surprise news events, for example—can easily double the volume of calls.

While it is uneconomical to staff in anticipation of these occurrences, Vanguard has found a way to cope with them without the serious deterioration in service quality experienced by many of its competitors. During these crisis periods, an investor may find herself giving a sell order over the phone to John Bogle, Vanguard's chief executive. He, and 300 other executives and middle managers, have for several years been trained and prescheduled to fill in immediately during crises. As a group, they are known as Vanguard's "Swiss Army," a reference to Switzerland's practice of counterbalancing a minimal standing army with an ability to mobilize rapidly and to arm a significant proportion of its population should a threat to national security arise. Just as this practice, and the periodic refresher training it requires, helps bring closer together Switzerland's diverse cultural groups, so it also puts dents into the wall between workers and managers at Vanguard.

At Mutual Benefit Life, different walls were breached by cross-training. As this company collapsed nineteen jobs into one, the barriers between the old narrow jobs, as well as the boundary lines around several departments, were obliterated to make work reengineering a reality.

Self-Control

Some companies are achieving even greater benefits by reinforcing front-line jobs with a third type of "steel"—*self-control*, or self-regulation.

If a job is given greater depth and its incumbent is equipped to shift from task to task as the needs of the customer or work require, what kind of supervision is then needed? Very little, or at least very little of what has traditionally been provided by the first-level supervisor or plant foreman. In an increasing number of companies, this traditional role has become an anachronism. As part of a plantwide restructuring, Union Carbide replaced most of its front-line supervisors in a Texas chemical plant with unionized hourly workers called "lead operators." Shell has made similar changes in some of its Canadian operations, and Procter & Gamble has had success replacing foremen with salaried technicians. AT&T, before it was broken up into several operating companies, had several years of good experience operating a 100-person specialized billing operation without any direct supervisors. Unionized employees had responsibility for ensuring service quality; providing training; improving productivity; managing operating and overhead expenses; monitoring attendance; and establishing administrative procedures.

These shifts are part of a widespread trend to erase what once was the first management level of many organization charts. Instead, the individual contributors are expected to take on more of the responsibility for their own direction and control. In some companies, this is called "employee empowerment," a phrase that, unfortunately, is more of an overused slogan than an indication of a reinforced job. The idea of empowerment—as in "I've empowered my subordinates to solve the problem for themselves"—has become a trendy way to express the age-old concept of delegation. It's often a good idea, but, as with delegation, it needs to be used selectively. Redesigning jobs so that a measure of ongoing self-control is built in requires more than the easy allusions to empowerment made by many contemporary managers.

Moving beyond the slogan stage requires ensuring that jobs are defined in terms of *outcomes*, expected results, rather than in terms of the usual laundry lists of tasks and activities that fill so many position descriptions. This is the starting point of self-regulation: It's hard to be in control of something when the something is vague or inexplicit. Then, along with a clearly communicated expectation that the job holder will do whatever is necessary to correct deviations from the expected outcome, must come ongoing direct feedback. For example, every job that bears upon customer satisfaction must be designed so that it includes *frequent, intimate* customer contact. How else can such work be kept whole other than by closing this performance/feedback cycle?

The same principle applies when the results of one employee's work become the input to, or are supportive of, another's. Short-term feedback is vital, but elaborate information systems are not necessarily required to deliver it. Farm equipment maker Deere & Company found that simply by juxtaposing operations that were once done in separate areas of the plant, both quality and productivity improved. Oil accumulators for Deere's tractor hydraulic systems were once welded far from the place in the plant where the systems were assembled. When they were tested after assembly, about 25 percent of the oil accumulators invariably leaked and had to be sent back for rewelding. A reengineering of the work process resulted in the welding and assembly jobs being placed next to each other. Thereafter, no foreman or quality inspector was needed to deal with the rework problem. When the first system failed, spraying the assembler with hydraulic fluid, the social process of mutual accommodation took hold (assembler to welder: "I'll kill you if this happens again"), and the welding problem disappeared.

Regardless which feedback mechanism is used, building self-control into jobs requires the elimination of the pockets of "information poverty" that have resulted from the Industrial Revolution-inspired work fragmentation. One traditionalist retailing executive used to justify his reliance on tight management of his store clerks by decomposing the word "supervision." He said it was important for his employees to realize how much they needed a boss with *super*-vision, the ability to see beyond their narrowly defined jobs to look at the whole picture of how the company made money by serving customers. He was right that such a perspective was vital to the business, but he was unaware of the way his narrow definition of the clerks' jobs generated much of the need for a role with this perspective. Reengineering the retail sales process and adding depth and flex to the clerks' work along the lines of the previous examples would force each clerk to have a start-to-finish view of what is required to satisfy a customer and an understanding of what must be done to contribute to this result.

Breaking out of this self-fulfilling pattern of narrow job definition and traditional supervision requires structural as well as informational changes. The old first-level supervisory jobs must *disappear* (not linger in the worker's shadow in some vaguely defined "advisory" capacity), and key elements of this job must migrate to the doers. These elements need to be chosen on a company-by-company basis but can typically include responsibility for issues such as:

- Work flow coordination
- Work and worker scheduling
- Productivity and quality assurance
- Continuous improvement of quality and productivity
- Orientation, training, and ongoing skill upgrading

Other aspects of this job, such as discipline, performance evaluation, and linkages with the rest of the company, are less downwardly delegatable. The need for them will not disappear in the new corporation, but the ways they are handled will change.

Composite Teams

There are limits to how much depth, flex, or self-control can be structured into any one job. Many work activities, especially after reengineering, are so broad that they cannot possibly be acomplished by any one individual. They frequently require more skills, integration, and coordination than are possible in a series of stand-alone jobs. Activities that test the boundaries of self-control may be more easily handled through peer pressure. In these situations, teams of individual contributors offer a good alternative to reinforced jobs as an organizational building block.

Teams are very trendy. As with many popular ideas, the word is often used without careful attention to which of its multiple meanings is most appropriate.

When some managers talk about the importance of teams, they are really talking about *teamwork*. This application of a group's best effort to pull together and accomplish something is important to all organizations. Few managers would do anything but exalt the virtues of teamwork, even though at the same time many preside over systems and management practices that favor individual over group accomplishment.

Types of Teams

Increasingly, employees are being asked to take time away from their individual assignments and to serve on task forces, committees, or teams. Texas Instruments has found it useful to create a hierarchy of teams that operate like a "shadow government" to help manage a semiconductor chip plant. Most powerful is a steering group made up of the plant manager and the heads of the factory's various functional units. It approves major projects and sets overall objectives. Subordinate to this steering group are teams responsible for either "corrective actions," "quality improvement," or "plant effectiveness." The corrective action groups are organized on an ad hoc basis to handle crises and problems that can quickly be solved, while the quality teams focus more on long-term improvements. Both types of teams oversee the effectiveness groups, made up of blue-collar production workers and individually contributing professionals. These groups are intended to help them stay coordinated.

The widespread use of these *part-time teams* is paralleled by an increased willingness to work around the problems of day-to-day corporate bureaucracy by assigning key tasks to *full-time special purpose* teams. As with the part-time groups that overlay the established bureaucracy, these teams usually include members from a cross section of functional departments. They have been especially useful as tools to speed development of new products. Chrysler's luxury sports car, the Viper, was developed by an eighty-five-person group—large for a team, but hundreds of people fewer than Detroit usually involves in launching a new vehicle.

The Viper team included members from engineering, manufacturing, and marketing, working alongside non-Chrysler employees on loan from key outside parts suppliers. Six of the members were unionized workers who, when the product development phase ended, were assigned to lead the teams of workers that will build each Viper. All eighty-five members were pulled away from their home base departments and worked together in one large open-plan room.

One of Chrysler's Detroit neighbors, Ford Motor Company, carried this idea one step further and used it to lower the wall separating it from Mazda, its partially owned Japanese partner. Over a five-year period, a new version of Ford's best-selling car, the Escort, was designed by a team with members from both companies. Initially, Ford's team members were to style the car's outside while Mazda's did the internal engineering, but soon the lines blurred as each side transferred know-how, as well as critical feedback, to the other.

Team-oriented efforts like these have been successful in many enterprises. But they all share a common failing. They are clever ways to *detour around*, instead of *addressing directly*, the problem of dysfunctional organization structures. Perhaps Chrysler recognized this when, in the wake of its success in rapidly developing the Viper, it pulled its engineers out of their functionally oriented departments, such as engine design, and moved them into teams that remain together for several years to plan a single model at a time. This shift alone saved Chrysler $500 million each year in costs associated with the design changes that result from each department taking the work of the previous one, adding its inputs and modifications, and sending the results to the next functional group. It also did away with the cumbersome matrix system of multiple bosses to whom each engineer had to account—a source of slowness and extra cost for many companies.

This Chrysler effort goes beyond employing the team just as an overlay or an add-on. It uses teams more as basic building blocks of the corporate structure. Examples of this type of team usage are few and far between, and some organizations that claim to operate this way have really just renamed their departments "teams." Hypothetically, an organization built around teams will have neither individual jobs nor functional departments—only teams, their members, and some limited management superstructure to keep everyone moving in roughly the same direction. Visions like this—bands of employees, all equals, and on the same electronic mail network, going off doing what the group consensus suggests is best for the enterprise—make for interesting speculation. But their fuzziness at times probably makes them better building blocks for a business novel than for a new corporation.

The *composite* team concept might serve as a middle ground between these romantic visions and the team-as-an-afterthought. Its members, like elements combined to form a new chemical compound, give up some of their individual identity and character for the good of the strength resulting from group cohesion. Like composite building materials, they are a balanced blend, in this case of functional skills and behavioral types. Indicators of management styles or personality types, such as the Myers-Briggs topology, are being increasingly used to calibrate this mix. Some companies compare their teams to DNA molecules and try to develop them so that each team entity includes most of the values and know-how necessary to function as a microcosm of the entire organization. Apple Computer has used this "genetic coding" model to plan for its long-term growth through spin-offs, each potentially able to replicate key factors behind the parent's success.

Teams and the Corporate Culture

Establishing successful teams can be difficult in some cultures. In nations like the United States, where individualism is a much stronger social value than collectivism, the tendency to talk about teams and team efforts is strong, but the results are frequently muddled. It is difficult to expect a company managed by business school graduates, whose education and careers have been built on their individual competitive successes, to provide unwavering support for a team-based organization.

One American school, the University of Tennessee's College of Business Administration, has worked hard to buck this trend. In a revamp of its M.B.A. curriculum, it made changes far beyond token acknowledgment of the usefulness of group efforts. Students there now study, work together, and take their examinations in teams. Grades are based primarily on their performance as team players. The school also realized this team orientation could not be successfully imposed on the "workers" while their "managers" (the faculty) operated under the old rules. So a team of ten professors, called the "A-Team," was created to teach jointly one unified first-year course, instead of ten individual ones. The content of the new curriculum stresses the overlapping and interdependent activities of a business and avoids the narrow functional specialization too common in both course catalogues and business school graduates' job descriptions.

Taking this idea a step further, several companies have built operations from the bottom up around teams. These include food retailers operating in bastions of American individualism, like Hannaford Brothers in Maine and Whole Foods Markets in Texas. In Whole Foods stores, departmental teams buy and price what they sell, functions seldom delegated to the store manager in most food chains. In both companies, teams do the hiring and firing, establish and monitor work rules, and have significant input into the compensation systems.

Using the group as the basic unit of organization is more common in countries like Japan, where well-entrenched cultural values favor group over individual identity. This is apparent in many Japanese organization charts, where only a handful of the most senior executive positions are specified. The remaining boxes invariably designate departments or sections, not individual managers or jobs. Japanese management tends to view the corporate structure in terms of hierarchically related collective units, not as a constellation of jobs. Relatively few national cultures have Japan's deeply ingrained emphasis on group effort and harmony. But the absence of this value is not necessarily a problem.

Some Japanese corporations are finding aspects of teams dysfunctional. Overreliance on groups as a basis of organization can limit individual creativity and smother deviant but potentially useful thinking. For these Japanese companies, the idea of the reinforced job may make more sense. Regardless, it is still possible in many cultures to selectively "engineer in" the most useful aspects of teams as organizational building blocks.

Collectively, composite teams possess the three attributes of an individual in a reinforced job. Their work has some requirement for *depth*. The team's overall mission requires more skill and knowledge than any single individual can possess. They also provide *flex*. While reinforced jobs bring multiple skills to bear on a task, composite teams allow for the possibility of a mix of disciplines and functional know-how, as well as job coverage for longer periods than any one individual could provide. Many of the tactics necessary to build *self-control* into individual jobs are useful with teams. Teams, when well-crafted, can also take advantage of the dynamics of social pressure and leadership to keep on course. Within limits, team members may impose discipline on their fellow workers, although to maintain cohesiveness they need an external manager to step in as needed. There is no such thing as a fully autonomous team operating successfully within a larger corporate structure. Some form of connection to the rest of the company is vital, not just to keep the team on course but also to allow it to function smoothly internally. Teams also tend to follow a life cycle; some are more mature than others and are able to take on more responsibility for self-control.

Nurturing Successful Teams

Well-functioning teams are created, not designated. When composites are made for use in construction, a considerable amount of energy is often required to fuse the raw materials together and to align them in a way that provides the structural strengths the builder is looking for. Similarly, composite teams require significant amounts of energy to guide their formation—much more than sending the new members to a session or two of team-building activities, and then calling them a team.

Team building is not something that happens in the abstract. Teams need to be built around three things: a *leader*, a *mission* or purpose, and the *attachments* that form among team members. If any of these is missing, the team's ability to serve as a structural building block is diminished. The pivotal role here is that of team leader, who gives the mission a sense of life by continually articulating and rearticulating it and who models the collaborative behavior necessary for effective functioning of the group.

This leader is not a disciplinarian and is not the one person in charge who is held accountable for all the team's actions. The role is more along the model developed in Roman times: *primus inter pares,* first among equals. Some companies, with especially mature teams, emphasize this by rotating this function. Others ensure the team members have a say in selecting their leader.

Much of the actual team building happens as the team members train together. Royal Dutch Shell required a half-year of individual training to produce a newly minted team member for its restructured chemical plant in Carrington, England. When Levi Strauss converted a New Mexico plant that made high-fashion jeans into a facility organized around self-managing teams, each sewing machine operator received 100 hours of instruction in topics ranging from labor cost reduction techniques to efficient ways to lay out equipment on the factory floor. The teams are also expected to provide regular feedback and suggestions to Levi's fashion designers about the ease of manufacturability of the new clothes they create.

Levi's operators must each perform at least three of what used to be individual jobs. At a highly automated Corning, Inc., ceramics plant, the requirement is more stringent: Team members must be proficient in three *families* of skills within two years of being hired, or they lose their jobs. Knowledge requirements like these are expensive. Between one and two days a week in the plant's first year of operation were devoted to worker training, both in technical and in teamworking skills.

As in reinforced jobs, the work given to a composite team must be complete. It needs to have a beginning and an end, rather than being the middle part of some elongated work flow. Packaging work this way allows the team to have a sense of *ownership* for its results. Levi's operators now each produce a finished garment, instead of spending their days sewing on only buttons or pockets. This ownership feeling is important psychologically, but it can have another, more vital purpose.

Before 1985, Japan Air Lines (JAL) organized its aircraft mechanics along the standard functional lines, with each maintenance group seeing dozens of planes over the course of a year. That year the worst air accident in history occurred when a JAL 747 crashed into a mountain in central Japan. All 520 people aboard died. While aviation safety investigators attributed the cause of the crash to a bulkhead improperly repaired many years before by the plane's manufacturer, JAL management was still very concerned that the absence of the necessary rivets had not been noticed by its mechanics, even though the plane had gone through several major maintenance overhauls since the omission. No one maintenance unit had overall ongoing responsibility for that particular plane.

To reduce the possibility of an oversight-driven accident happening again, JAL reorganized the maintenance groups. Each fifteen-person team, called a *kizuki* (which means "plane-crazy," an indication of the attachments that form between worker and work), is assigned one 747 and one DC-10 from the JAL fleet. The team has complete responsibility for the operability of these planes. Members' signatures appear on a special plaque inside each plane's passenger cabin. After a major aircraft repair, the maintenance team leader is its first passenger.

Additional Economic Benefits of Composite Teams

Composite teams create significant opportunities for *leverage*. Consider the experience of Teli, a Swedish telecommunications equipment maker, in rethinking the way it produces computer software. Writing software is generally an economic black hole. Costs predictably escalate from original estimates, and deadlines are faint hopes, never solid commitments. Most software writing is done by an individual college-trained engineer who stays with a project from start to finish. These engineers enjoy exercising creativity as they generate computer code, but few like the drudgery of fully documenting their efforts, making it difficult to fix mistakes, install updates, or cope with programmer turnover.

Teli's repackaging of this work involved creation of a team with three levels of talent, all working together as close partners. A seasoned software writer serves as team leader and devotes most of his or her time to specifying the functionality each segment of the computer program needs and monitoring its development. Two junior programmers break down the work even further into self-contained modules, which are then written, documented, and tested by four workers whose previous factory assembly jobs had been taken over by robots. This structure creates an upward skill path for the formerly dead-ended factory workers and results in high-quality software being produced much faster and more economically than it could with the solo engineer approach.

Other significant *economies* are possible when the team is used as the basic element of organization. They come from a combination of cross-utilization and reduced management overhead. Arnold Donald, head of a Monsanto division, likes to restructure work so a team of three people does the work of five stand-alone employees. To maintain equity, the team is paid the wages of four regular workers. At eight General Mills plants, work has been restructured to be done in teams where every worker is expected to learn how to do every step in the manufacturing process as well as to troubleshoot machine malfunctions and workload bottlenecks. Team members participate in selecting a leader from their membership. The leaders then report directly to the plant supervisor, allowing for the elimination of four intervening layers of middle managers.

Similar savings are possible in service-oriented jobs. At Aetna Life & Casualty Company, organizing around teams allowed its previous one-to-seven ratio of middle managers to workers to become one-to-thirty—a more than fourfold reduction!

Load-Bearing Managers

Composite teams and reinforced jobs reduce the *quantity* of managers a company requires. This must happen, or the ability of the job holders and the team members to be self-governing will be needlessly constrained, many anticipated cost savings will never be realized, and the company will never achieve the goal of minimizing its internal walls. *Each management position on an organization chart marks the location of a wall,* as defined by the turf the manager is given responsibility for. But even more significant, use of these organizational building blocks also dictates several *qualitative* changes in the middle manager's role.

While it might be relatively easy to assert that the job of the traditional front-line supervisor needs to disappear as its responsibilities migrate to individuals or teams, it is harder to specify a single new role appropriate for all remaining managers. An old story, still making the rounds at many management conferences, typifies some of these difficulties. It goes something like this: "The factory (or company) of the future will be staffed very leanly: one man and one dog. The man will be there to feed the dog. The dog will be there to make sure the man doesn't touch the machines."

While the story usually gets a hearty round of laughs, the mentality behind it—and the lack of a well-defined positive role for the middle manager—is sadly alive and well in many corporate restructurings. Chapter 11 fills some of this vacuum by laying out several viable ways middle managers can operate in the leanly structured new corporation. While these configurations are lean, they are still *structures* and as such must be expected to bear *loads.*

One of the most important things a building's structure does is channel the loads imposed on the building to the ground. These loads are partly caused by the building's weight and partly a result of the external pressures it experiences. The structure must be able to direct both of these constructively, or the building cannot stand.

Similarly, the key elements of an organization must be capable of channeling pressures from a variety of directions. Employee needs, customer wants, and owner requirements all must be kept in some sort of balanced state. These forces also have to be reconciled with the demands made by the corporation's other stakeholders. Strong teams and reinforced jobs can do just so much of this and stay focused on their work at hand. Performing much of this multifaceted balancing feat is the job of the company's management structure, including the middle managers.

The corporate structure must bear loads in at least two dimensions—it needs to provide the company with both horizontal and vertical stability. In the *horizontal* dimension, the various teams, cross-functional processes, and reinforced jobs need a measure of orchestration. Ways of organizing for this are the subject of Chapters 7 and 8.

Hierarchy will not disappear in the new corporation. But it will be tamed, each of its *vertical* tiers will have a distinct rationale, and increased options will be built into its upward careerflow. These reforms are detailed in Chapters 9 and 10.

The Danger of Fragmentation

Before moving on, it is worth highlighting a problem that seriously limits the load-bearing ability of many middle-management positions. It is fragmentation, another vestige of the organizational mentality spawned by the Industrial Revolution. Reinforced jobs and composite teams fight *work* fragmentation; management positions, if they are to be effective building blocks, must minimize *role* fragmentation.

Just as fault lines and impurities hinder the performance of building materials, management work is negatively affected when it is polluted with nonmanagement responsibilities. It is also harmed when too many artificial distinctions are made between managers and those managed.

Managers in the new corporation need to be separate but not apart from those they are managing. This is not possible if the manager is also doing the work of an individual contributor.

In studies pioneered by General Electric and replicated in dozens of other companies, most middle managers were found to be spending very significant amounts of time performing tasks that had little to do with their management role. A number of these managers devoted from half to three-quarters of their time to these activities, which explains why they had time to oversee only three or four subordinates. Most of this nonmanagerial work could probably have been delegated to their subordinates. Some of it was directly intertwined with the subordinates' own work, thus fragmenting both the manager's and the workers' jobs and leading sometimes to oversupervising the workers (because the manager is always in the thick of their responsibilities) and also frequently to undermanaging them.

Many managers, when also allowed to be part-time individual contributors, seem to never develop their talents in directing, monitoring, coaching, and developing others. It is easier, when performance problems or workload crises emerge, just to do it all themselves. Sometimes it is also more fun. The tasks these managers "scoop upward" tend to be the most interesting and motivating as well as most likely to be noticed and to receive recognition. This, when coupled with closer-than-necessary supervision, is a formula guaranteed to demotivate employees.

R. Roosevelt Thomas, a leading expert in managing diversity, has seen the same pattern, which he calls the Doer Model of Management, in companies that have difficulties assimilating immigrants, minorities, and women into their work forces. He believes managers should be managing people, not doing the business. He observes that "Doer managers love to be in the trenches. It keeps them out of the line of fire."

Full-time load-bearing managers receive premium pay for staying in the line of fire. But that does not mean living in a world apart from those managed. Unfortunately, for almost 200 years, managers have accumulated perks and prerogatives that have created wide chasms between them and those whose work they oversee.

Minimizing these barriers has been a primary objective of many successful organizers, from Mao Tse-tung to Sam Walton. Mao, the builder of one of the world's largest military forces, implored his officers to

> Live under the same conditions as their men, for that is the only way they can gain from their men the admiration and confidence so vital in war. . . . Thus we may attain the unification of the officer and soldier groups, a unity both horizontal within the group itself, and vertical, that is, from lower to higher echelons. It is only when such unity is present that units can be said to be powerful combat factors.

A similar wisdom also has been articulated by astute capitalists. Sam Walton, the founder of the world's largest retail company, speculates in his autobiography that many companies might perform much better economically if their executives' life-styles were a little closer to those of their average customers or employees.

For some industries, this issue relates as much to concerns about strategic decision making as to beliefs about social equity. For years, executives at some U.S. automakers lived in a world far apart from that inhabited by their customers, at least regarding their automobiles. Annually, or more often, they had their choice of their company's products delivered from the factory to their front door. These vehicles often received special attention as they were built to ensure they were problem-free. After the executive drove the car to the office, a company employee would take the keys and give the car its daily washing, refueling, and preventive maintenance inspection.

While for many years these practices were rationalized as an executive "perk," necessary because the executive was an ambassador of the company, they also very effectively shut off the key decision makers in these centralized, top-down companies from timely, direct experience with the quality, economy, and reliability problems their customers encountered each day. And while their tendency to drive only their own company's products signaled loyalty, it also insulated them from direct contact with the advances being made by their Asian and European competitors.

Increasingly, steps are being taken, at least concerning middle management work styles, to minimize some of the social walls that have divided blue- and white-collar auto employees. At Honda's plants in Marysville, Ohio, and at General Motors' Spring Hill, Tennessee, Saturn complex, it is impossible to tell the plant manager from the car builders by either dress or where they eat lunch. At Spring Hill, the air-conditioning system includes the factory as well as the offices, and the same attention that ensured ergonomic design of the manager's office furniture also made sure the assembly-line floor was made of wood. Wood is more comfortable than concrete, and worker comfort reduces fatigue-induced mistakes, believes the G.M. plant manager.

Mars, Inc., the $12 billion global candy maker, goes even further than G.M.'s Saturn. No employee, including the chief executive of this family-owned business, has a private office. He sits in the back corner of a huge room, sharing a secretary with two others, in a setting less elegant than the back rooms of many Wall Street brokerages. All employees handle their own phone calls, make their own copies, and are separated from each other by no more than five pay grades. Mars also maintains an exemplary profit-sharing program that reinforces the common ties between managers and individual contributors. Other successful, growth-oriented multinationals, such as Du Pont, Merck, and PepsiCo,

Figure 7. The reshaping process (1).

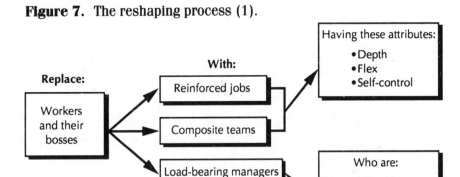

have lessened hierarchical fragmentation and helped ensure that role differences in the organizations were load-bearing, not status-bearing, by making a common executive compensation practice—stock option awards—available to all employees.

Reinforced jobs, composite teams, and load-bearing managers are the basic building blocks of the new corporation (see Figure 7). They can serve as the basis for an organization that is fast, flexible, and focused. They provide the all-important foundation for the innovative organization structures that are emerging to carry businesses into the first century of globally based competition.

It can be perilous to ignore the interplay between structures and the materials they are built from. Successful organization reshaping starts with careful decisions about *what* is being structured. What is the nature of the boxes that the lines are to connect? Exactly what kinds of jobs, teams, and managers are most appropriate? How can they best be reinforced, utilize a composite of strengths, and bear loads? And how can they survive in a business environment that increasingly looks like an ocean of shifting sand?

Chapter 7
Structure Horizontally

Let form follow function: Turn the organization
on its side for fast and easy movement.

Let's take stock of where we are. Quick-fix downsizings and fad-driven reorganizations have been rejected. Over time they seldom achieve their objectives, often do more harm than good, and are difficult to sustain.

Designing a new corporation requires a top-down refocusing around the capabilities most critical to future success and a closely linked bottom-up reconsideration of the activities and processes vital to this focus.

Then, keyed to the results of this grass-roots effort to build speed, simplicity, and balance into the company, comes a careful selection of the type of jobs, teams, and oversight needed from which the new corporation can be built.

With these as the basic structural materials, choices now can be made about how they can be best configured.

As mentioned in Chapter 1, it has become fashionable to minimize the importance of these choices. Structure is frequently branded as an "unnecessary evil." In architectural design work, though, the idea of structure has fewer negative connotations. Let's consider what part structure plays in the design of buildings and see if it can provide analogous benefits to organizations.

What Structure Does

Structure is what makes a building stand up. It defines the kinds of space that are available within it. The shape it designates should also enable the building to serve the purpose for which it was constructed. And the appearance of some structures is significantly aesthetically pleasing for them to be considered works of art—an end in themselves, apart from whatever functionality they provide.

Structures Bear Loads

When you look at a building, it generally appears very still. But the achievement of this motionless state requires a considerable degree of careful planning. Actually a lot is going on just to keep the building still. From a structural engineer's point of view, a building is a beehive of activity, with an array of strong, potentially disruptive forces being generated by the weight of the building itself, its occupants, their furniture, and their equipment. The building also experiences a variety of acute forces caused by winds, snow, ice, and possibly earthquakes. A third category of pressures, slower to act but just as potentially disruptive, includes those generated by the uneven settlement of the land beneath the structure and the seasonal changes in air temperature.

For the building to remain static, each of these forces must be resisted by an equal, but opposite, reactive force. This principle, first articulated by Isaac Newton, mandates that the load-bearing elements in a structure must provide a bridge between the acting and the reacting pressures, between, for example, the weight of the roof and the upward pressure exerted by the building's foundation to resist it. The net result is the achievement of a state of dynamic equilibrium, masquerading as a still, erect building.

Corporations also must be able to achieve a dynamic equilibrium. Their structures have to facilitate the balancing of many internally and externally induced forces and the counterpressures that arise because of them. At the enterprise level, a dynamic balance must be achieved among the wants of the business's owners, its employees, and its customers. It must achieve a measure of workable adaptation to the demands of its regulators, as well as to the needs of its supplier-partners. Within the company, the attractiveness of long product runs to factory managers must be measured against the hope of the sales force for an offering that can be customized to each buyer's requirements. And the reluctance of the sales people to ask for prompt payment must be balanced with the sleepless nights experienced by the accounting manager as past-due receivables age.

These, and many other pressures, create priorities for the organization structure. Tremendous time and energy are often required to cope with them, although in the end this may go unnoticed because, as with the "motionless" building, nothing seems to have changed. Pure survival usually occurs without a lot of fanfare.

Structures Define Space

A building is a container of space. Its form defines, as well as confines, space. Space behaves the way fluids do. It can be like a still and motionless pond or a rapidly moving river current. It can seem bottled up and trapped or free-flowing and chaotic. These two types of space, static and dynamic, are direct results of the structural envelope around them.

Some organization planners use models that allow them to think carefully about the kind of space they are creating. Some may use the architectural metaphor and think of a corporate structure as if it were a house with many rooms inside, each representing a department or division. The house may have many levels, some split, and several wings, each running off in a different direction. Planners consider in detail the activities occurring in each room and are very deliberate about which "rooms" are placed where, how small or large the openings are between them, and where the staircases are placed to allow for vertical movement.

High ceilings, wide open doorways, and large picture windows all contribute to the sensation of a dynamic physical space. What would be their organizational counterpart?

The kind of space of most concern to organization designers is *interaction space.* Who needs to see or talk to whom most often? What perspectives should most frequently intermingle? What aspects of the company's operations work best when left alone? Changing organization structure alone seldom is sufficient to solve all communication problems, but structure that is planned without regard to the barriers it raises can quickly be self-defeating. Think about all the organizational walls that had to be surmounted just to bring together car designers and car engineers in General Motors' old structure. Compare this with Chrysler's Team Viper, all working together in one organization unit, housed in a large room. Contrast the barriers that separate most manufacturers from direct contact with their customers with the "interaction space" created when the German farm equipment maker Claas added a small retail component to its organization structure.

Claas uses the interactions that occur between its customers and its employees in these stores as a window into the customers' minds, providing unfiltered feedback about product quality and an early alert to changing buyer needs. Architects use the same technique to create dynamic space; they put windows inside buildings to reduce feelings of confinement and facilitate informal communication.

While there are almost countless structural variations and architectural styles (such as Classical, Romanesque, Gothic, Renaissance, Baroque, Bauhaus, Modern, and Postmodern), several contemporary American architects found they could simplify matters by classifying most structures into one of three types: skeletal, planar, and plastic. Each type occurs throughout architectural history; each has a strikingly different form.

Skeletal buildings are easy to spot. As the American architects note: "Their bones show." Paris's Notre Dame Cathedral and Athens's Parthenon illustrate this effect, as does the Eiffel Tower. Another example is the modernist buildings designed by Mies van der Rohe for the Illinois Institute of Technology, as well as his famed Seagram Building in Manhattan. Their steel beams and columns are the most visually striking things about them.

Some corporate structures reflect aspects of this skeletal orientation. In the early twentieth century, the tightly compartmentalized organizations created by Theodore Vail for AT&T and by Alfred Sloan for General Motors gave military-style importance to structural level and the rank it designated. Over time, structures like these grew by excessive fragmentation and became more like government bureaucracies than like private enterprises. The space created by these structures tends to be very confining and static.

The *planar* form gives great emphasis to one distinct horizontal or vertical element that defines the structure. It might be a floor, a ceiling, or a wall. Some Oriental architecture uses this form, as do many of Frank Lloyd Wright's houses, especially Fallingwater (see page 109). The dramatic appearance of Eero Saarinen's Dulles Airport terminal outside Washington, D.C., results from a skillful application of the planar structure in the giant curved roof.

This structure's organizational counterparts are those companies with tightly integrated configurations—companies that are able to say, "Everything we sell, we make; everything we make, we design; and every raw material we use, we mine, refine, or find." This was once the model for success in a number of industries. Railroads made much of their rolling stock, the telephone company made all the telephones, Ford made the steel used in its cars, some supermarket giants processed much of the food they sold, and the U.S. military produced most of its armaments in government-owned arsenals. It is a good organizational strategy in times of monopoly or scarcity; what better way to have access to supply than to own it? But it is less relevant in a time of intense competition among suppliers and the emergence of global markets for so many raw materials and components.

Planar structures provide for a more dynamic space than do skeletal ones. But their integrated nature usually channels the flow in one direction. It is hard to listen to an oil industry veteran talk about the business for longer than a minute or two without the words "upstream" or "downstream" entering the conversation.

The third generic structural form, *plastic,* is the architect's equivalent of sculpture. Plastic buildings use a variety of geometric shapes—cubes, pyramids, domes, spheres, cylinders—and the geometry is what is most noticed, not the load-bearing skeleton or the horizontal or vertical dimensions. For architectural examples, go to Istanbul to see the Hagia Sophia, a model of flexibility: once a cathedral, then a mosque, now a museum. Visit I. M. Pei's pyramidal entrance at the Louvre. Or, when attending a management development program at the Harvard Business School, walk across the Charles River and look at the distinctive "unbuildinglike" appearance of Larsen Hall on the campus of the Harvard Graduate School of Education.

Plasticity, as an organizational form, is becoming increasingly popular. It is a way to combine free-form space with an element of structural rigor. Johnson & Johnson and 3M have had many decades of experience organizing with this flexible form. Kyocera Corporation, a $3-billion-a-year maverick Japanese manufacturer based in Kyoto, structures itself similarly. This configuration is not limited to high-tech businesses, though. A maker of products as mundane as nails, screws, and bolts—the Illinois Tool Works—favors this form to keep its arms around its ninety small divisions.

Plastic structures produce dynamic space. Their lack of boxiness, or linearity, can provide many paths for movement and communication. Too many, in some cases, if the structure grows too large.

Three types of structures; three types of space enclosed. One fragmented, one tightly integrated, the other fluid and flexible. What the new corporation needs most is an ample measure of the fluid and flexible.

Structures Look Good

In architecture, appearance counts. Most buildings do a good job supporting their loads, and many deal with space well. But relatively few become memorable as enduring works of art.

Although this is not always freely admitted, corporate structures also can serve a "higher purpose" beyond their functional, economic utility. Some philosophers look to a people's art and buildings to find an expression of their morality. They can also look to the kinds of organization structures that have been created. Just as a building designed only for its immediate usefulness might be considered merely another machine, so might an organization planned solely to be economically efficient. To the extent a company's economic performance occurs as a result of, not in spite of, its attention to some higher aspirations, it has a greater chance of being in sync with the overall society upon which it depends and of growing in harmony with that society.

These "higher aspirations" are many and varied. In companies like Mexico's Grupo Industrial Alfa and Brazil's Brastemp S.A. and in many struggling start-ups in Eastern Europe, the hope is to contribute to and to share in the rewards of a rapidly modernizing economy. Raymond Ackerman has built Pick 'n Pay Stores Ltd. into more than just Africa's largest food retailer. Its structure is one that has for many years accelerated the development of a nonracial management team, charting a path a number of other South African-based world-class enterprises are following. The intense drive behind many of Japan's and Germany's post-World War II businesses was fueled by a motivation to rebuild their nations and to demonstrate the positive role they could play in the world's economy. Gilbert Trigano's Club Med, a French postwar start-up, was structured as more than an all-inclusive, sport-oriented vacation provider. Its organization chart includes a place for customers as well as for staff, with only minimal walls between each, reinforcing a cultural aspiration for a more egalitarian world.

In addition to reflecting some important higher mission, good structures must also meet criteria reflecting individual needs. At the least, they should not place obstacles in the way of their employees' good physical and psychological health. Their methods of providing for recognition and advancement should not make disappointment and demotivation reasonable expectations for most employees. Their concerns for efficiency and their intolerance for waste should be broad enough to include awareness of misused talents and underperforming human potential.

As companies that address these issues show, "looking good" can be important to sustained business success, and it needs to be more than skin deep. It has to be reflected throughout the structure, not just added on as a community affairs, employee assistance, or organization development departmental appendage.

New Structures for New Strategies

What kind of corporate structures are best at dealing with these concerns about strength, space, and spirit? We need some new principles of organization design, some borrowed and adapted from architecture.

The most frequently espoused principle, common to both design realms, is the old adage about form needing to follow function. This principle is usually attributed to Louis Sullivan, the Chicago architect who pioneered the use of steel frame construction in a city in great need of new buildings to replace a downtown gutted by a disastrous fire. Sullivan took advantage of a newly developed material, structural steel, and made use of a new technology for moving people from floor to floor (the Otis elevator) to design a number of the Chicago Loop's most significant buildings.

Today's organizational architects face a situation not unlike Sullivan's. More than a decade of financial restructuring and downsizing have gutted the original logic behind many corporate structures. That is the bad news. The good news is that a powerful combination of new building blocks (reinforced jobs, composite teams, and load-bearing managers) and enabling technologies (new, computer-supported information and telecommunications techniques) is making possible new forms of organization. Adoption of new ideas is seldom easy and straightforward. Necessity is usually more powerful than trendiness, and the necessity to accommodate strategies of focus, flexibility, and speed is fueling a reexamination of traditional organization structures. Several attributes seem most important to consider as organization structures are reshaped.

Pointedness

How focused is the structure on what it takes to succeed in its particular industry? Do at least two-thirds of the activities it provides support critical or cutting-edge capabilities? While many companies feel this is something that can be taken for granted, audits of how resources are allocated to capabilities usually discover that three-quarters or more are devoted to either core or complementary skills, those that neither directly serve the customer nor are the basis for today's competitive advantage. Resource concentrations are usually good clues about the direction a business is taking. Having them match the competitive dynamics of the industry is one of the greatest sources of strength the organization structure can provide.

Scale

How big is the organization? Size is measured not just by counting heads, but by measuring fragmentation. An organization of 1,000 employees with only 50 individual jobs is "smaller" than one with the same number of workers but 500 different ways to divide responsibilities.

Regardless of how it is measured, overall organization size is a critical concern. Many Japanese companies are given excessive praise for their ability to coordinate diverse functions, create new knowledge, and quickly turn that knowledge into on-the-shelf products. But what is sometimes forgotten as Japanese management practices are imitated is that many of these companies are much smaller than their Western counterparts. NEC's Japan-based work force only numbers 37,000; Kao, in businesses ranging from cosmetics to computer disks, has fewer than 7,000 employees. As size increases, the number of possible interactions increases at an even faster rate, adding to the load on the structure.

This pressure is usually managed by increased subdivision, which again creates new problems of coordination and information transfer. Instead, more attention is needed to create what some call an organization with the clout of a giant and the nimbleness of an elf. The trick is to keep the organization sufficiently small and focused, so that a minute division of labor is unnecessary. The structure should be designed so that users and providers are as close together as possible and so that sequential transfers of responsibility among organization units are minimized or eliminated. Companies like Johnson & Johnson and Microsoft are good followers of these principles. Microsoft keeps business units to a 200-person maximum, the limit its founder, Bill Gates, feels allows most people to know each other by name and not have their contributions lost in an overly fragmented accountability structure.

The giant/elf sleight-of-hand is possible if it is accompanied by work resizing, both top down and bottom up. The smaller scale of operations this permits, in turn, makes it possible to create a structure that *minimizes the distance from any job in it to the company's outside environment*, so that a greater percentage of every employee's time is spent interacting with customers, suppliers, or others with information about events outside the company instead of focusing attention on intracompany gossip and internal policies. Visualizing a resized company as a geometric figure shows a structure that has maximized its external surface area in relation to its volume. Organizationally speaking, the white space on its chart has been minimized.

Permeability

Having a lot of surface area is one thing; ensuring that information and ideas flow across that surface is something else. A good organization boundary is one that is porous, or at least semipermeable. At the company's external boundary, there needs to be an easy blending with the outside environment.

This idea can be appreciated if you visualize a building or a house that seems to fit almost seamlessly into its environment. Fallingwater is a good example. The strong horizontal lines of its exterior structure and the cascading effect of its multiple levels as they seem to float above each other is the stone and concrete equivalent of the stream and waterfall above which it is built. Its designer, Frank Lloyd Wright (who was Louis Sullivan's apprentice), believed that if a house is to be built atop a hill, it should appear to be *of* the hill, not just placed *on* it. In Germany's Swabian Alps, the castle of the Hohenzollerns was so well-sited on a mountain peak that its multitowered shape appears to complete the mountain's silhouette, instead of doing what it actually does, which is to dominate the valley below.

A similar impression is apparent throughout the countryside of Japan, where many Buddhist temples seem to be an integral part of the natural environment, rather than set out to dominate it. Instead of imposing themselves on the environment, these pagodas have a structure, consisting of a central post with a series of roofs piled up around it, that is not unlike the stem and branches of a tree and that is as effective as a tree in surviving the earthquakes common in Japan. This design, and other wood-frame structures, may appear weak, but they are able to ride out many movements of the earth that would lead to the collapse of stronger-appearing stone buildings.

Just as nature and architecture meet in these noted buildings, organization and environment must in the new corporation. The company's form must allow for easy, complementary connections with the outside world, as well as with the internal functionality that has traditionally governed corporations. This is the best way to ensure that the business will survive the hard-to-anticipate shocks and tremors that are accompanying the globalization of many industries.

Flowing Space

When alternative organization structures are being considered, the best choice is frequently the one that allows for space that flows, or dynamic space. These tend to be planar or plastic structures. These structures, especially the plastic ones, are best at minimizing the distance between two points—or people—who need to be linked. Many elaborate mechanisms are available to facilitate communications—global telecommunications, computer-facilitated meetings, electronic and voice mail, videoconferencing. But before investing in these intriguing but costly technologies, doesn't it make sense first to look for ways to minimize your company's need for them?

The shortest distance between two points is not necessarily a straight line. When thinking about organizational communication,

Fallingwater, Frank Lloyd Wright's award-winning house atop Bear Run in western Pennsylvania, is a source of many ideas for organizational architects.

Its horizontal shape permits large, multipurpose rooms and easy circulation of people and light—just as horizontally oriented organizations can speed work flows and allow ideas to move easily across the business.

Fallingwater is designed to blend with its environment, not overpower it, just as many companies are trying to build partnerships with their customers and suppliers, rather than treating them as adversaries to overcome.

Fallingwater allows its inhabitants to see easily the woods surrounding it and hear the sound of the waterfall below; well-designed organizations minimize barriers between those working within them and the markets they serve.

Photo by Thomas A. Heinz, courtesy of Western Pennsylvania Conservancy.

"shortest" is not so much a geographic concept as one related to speed and effort. Short paths are those that can be transversed the quickest, with the least expenditure of effort. In organization hierarchies the most difficult paths are frequently those that go up or down the hierarchy, the chain of command. These paths are too congested with concerns about authority, accountability, dependency, evaluation, leadership, and status to serve as especially effective communication conduits.

Instead, in most corporations, information—and rumors—tend to flow fastest *across* the hierarchy, from peer to peer. These are the natural channels of "least effort." Instead of starting out by resisting them with technological fixes, it can make sense to let nature take its course and design structures that maximize the ratio of peers to managers.

In building architecture, the key flows to be managed are the movements of the structure's inhabitants, light, air, and—for aesthetic reasons—the eye as it scans the building. At Fallingwater, Wright influenced these flows by accentuating the house's horizontal dimension and by locating large windows in places that allow those inside to see the outdoors at the same time they glance across a room. In much of his architecture, he also minimized the use of right angles and used building materials native to the site, all techniques that minimize obstacles to free movement and create the feeling that the occupant is part of some space larger than that the structure defines.

Of these design tactics, probably the most powerful is the use of the horizontal. Less energy and effort is required to move in the horizontal dimension than in the vertical. The energy required to walk up a fifteen-foot flight of steps would provide for many more feet of distance covered if the travel were limited to one level. The lesson here for organization structure is to minimize the levels or, better put, to minimize the vertical height of the structure in favor of its horizontal expanse.

Easy flow is also that which happens rapidly. In Japanese gardens the best views are often obtained by staying on the path defined by the stone steps that meander through them. Some gardens deliberately vary the spacing between the steps to either speed up or slow down the visitor, depending on how interesting the garden is from a particular vantage point on the path. Closely spaced stones require short, slow steps, while a broader spacing encourages more rapid movement.

The same principle holds for what goes on within horizontal organizational turf. The more the organization is subdivided—by departments, narrowly defined jobs, or teams floating free from the rest of the organization—the longer it takes for important interactions to occur and for information and ideas to circulate. To reduce delays in information flow, minimize these subdivisions; turn the organization on its side.

Chapter 8

Organize Around Customers and Processes

Organize around cross-cutting processes, not functional fiefdoms.

Ideas from the realm of architectural design, such as those discussed in Chapter 7, are starting to appear in organization structures throughout the world. There are a number of new directions being taken. Here are some of the more promising ones and the lessons that can be drawn from them.

New Forms of Organizational Structures

Spin-Offs

The practice of *spinning off* a piece of a larger corporation became common in the 1980s and has continued to be popular even after many of the financial mechanisms of that decade that served as a restructuring lubricant disappeared. Spin-offs were once done primarily to benefit the parent company's stock price; now they are more commonly used to achieve operational improvements.

Casting off portions of a corporation is a useful strategic tool. It is often a good way to resize a business around the capabilities that make the most sense competitively. It is also a helpful organizational tool to use to reshape a company to reach its optimum size. Managers and employees tend to behave differently in smaller, more focused entities. The president of a defense contractor that was formerly a division of a larger business observed: "We became much more aggressive when we were measured and rewarded on things that we could control." John Langford, an executive vice-president of Vista Chemical Company, once a part of Du Pont, observed that complaints about being in a commodities business are really just excuses for being part of a corporate structure that forces you to lose contact with your customers, what they most value and are willing to pay a premium price for. Having the right scale can open up many new possibilities for competing.

There can be many benefits in changing from being part of a planar structure to an independent, more plastic form. An example is the exploration and production division of Sun Oil, which was spun off as the Oryx Energy Company. Named after the fast African antelope, Oryx quickly became the largest U.S. independent producer of gas and oil. When part of Sun, it emphasized finding oil to supply its parent's refineries. But as an independent, it followed its own intuition about where its industry was moving. Noticing that increasing environmental concerns were likely to favor gas as an energy source over oil, Oryx fueled its own growth by giving greater emphasis to natural gas exploration.

IBM has moved a step in this direction, using the spin-off idea as a basis for reorganizing parts of the $65 billion corporation into more than a dozen semiautonomous businesses. Several of these are software businesses, which, like Oryx, may be able to use the separation from what has been a hardware-driven company to achieve more of their own potential.

Several smaller companies that may aspire to IBM-like reputations in their marketplaces are trying to avoid the splitting IBM found necessary by undertaking to grow in sales, not in bulk. Cypress, a Silicon Valley semiconductor maker, makes a point of keeping new product lines away from its existing organization. Instead, each is handed off to a separate start-up venture, along with up to 19 percent of the venture's stock, which is owned by its employees. The rest of the ownership remains with the parent. Cypress's chief executive, T. J. Rodgers, explains: "I would rather see our billion-dollar company of the 1990s be ten $100 million companies, all strong, growing, healthy, and aggressive as hell." No tall, vertical pyramids here. For Rogers, the only alternative is an aging billion-dollar business that "spends more time defending its turf than growing."

Partnerships

Joint ventures are an increasingly popular way to get around the limitations of an existing corporate structure. In addition to its strategy of structural subdivision, IBM has formed partnerships or alliances with a surprisingly broad array of other companies—Apple, Intel, Mitsubishi, Motorola, Siemens, Toshiba, and Wang. Many of these are also strong marketplace competitors of IBM. Ford has also learned that rivals can be allies. By teaming up on focused projects with Mazda, Nissan, and Volkswagen, it is able to field a much broader product line than would be possible if it were to follow a "go-it-alone" approach to the global marketplace. And Corning Glass Works has stayed focused on refining its critical capabilities in optical fiber production by letting six joint ventures carry the weight of building a sales and marketing capability for these products in Europe and in the Far East.

In some situations, the best basis for collaborative links is around information. *Information partnerships* can be a creative way for one company to share the scale of another. Information sharing was the basis for the recoupling of dozens of small, specialized Italian textile companies created when several large family-owned conglomerates were broken apart.

Wal-Mart, the world's largest retailer, has taken a focused approach to creating information partnerships with its various constituencies. It links itself to the concerns of many of its U.S. customers with a procurement policy emphasizing "Buy American," a policy that is highlighted in advertising and store signage. It has also pushed the use of technology to its fullest by using electronic data interchange to release sales figures regularly to the makers of the products it sells, who are then expected to replenish Wal-Mart's inventory automatically. In addition to reducing inventory size, this procedure eliminates the need for middlemen, such as merchandise brokers and independent sales representatives, who formerly were the human links in this information flow.

Visa, the world's largest credit card brand, is another example of the new corporate forms emerging from the electronic information network revolution. Called a *reverse holding company* by Dee Hock, its founder, it is owned by its 22,000 member banks and by other financial institutions. Built on innovation, it created the first system for banks to transfer money electronically to each other. Visa serves as a good model of an intermediary organization that can allow companies to extend their boundaries without adding a cumbersome hierarchy.

Contrast Visa's success as a focused federation with the "go-it-alone" attempt of United Airlines to build one monolithic organization that offered all the key services needed by a business traveler. Its short-lived Allegis Corporation attempted to put under one hierarchical roof the operations of the airline, Hertz car rentals, and Westin hotels, along with an automated reservation system linking all three. This conglomeration failed, partially because of Wall Street skepticism that managerial synergies would really emerge; the financial markets doubted that an executive from a successful car rental agency would be able to contribute much operational wisdom to help the airline grow its business.

The Visa network took off only when it was spun free from one of the network's nodes, its parent Bank of America. *Groupings that seem logical because of information commonness can suffer when placed in a relationship based on hierarchal ownership. Flow happens best horizontally, not up and over.* Two Harvard Business School professors, Benn Konsynski and Warren McFarlan, say this well when they observe: "Managers from companies in reciprocal industries should now be plotting common approaches to customers through relational data bases, not plotting how to take each other over."

The Organizational Amoeba

Audrey Freedman, a labor economist and an astute observer of changes in corporate form, likens many emerging corporate structures to the basic biological organism, the amoeba. This unicellular microscopic animal, a prototype of the plastic structure, is almost constantly changing its shape. It is impossible for an amoeba to move without reorganizing itself. It ingests food not through a designated mouth, but by extending an armlike portion of its body toward whatever has stimulated its interest. The food is then surrounded, covered with cellular material, engulfed by the organism, and circulated around to the portions of it needing nourishment.

The amoeba grows by mitosis, the division of one amply nourished cell into two. This is not unlike Illinois Tool Works' growth strategy. The company actively extends feelers to find market niches where it can be the dominant player. Then it stays so close to its customers (perhaps engulfing their ideas for product improvement) that its engineers or marketers discover a new need and invent a solution. Then comes the corporate mitosis; the new product, and its associated employees, are spun off as a new entity. Its current divisions include the world's largest maker of plastic buckles and the inventor of the plastic loops that hold six-packs of beer and soda together. Both entities resulted from this spinning-off process.

Health-care products giant Johnson & Johnson follows the same logic. When the endoscopic (small-incision surgery) portion of one of its 160-odd companies showed significantly greater growth potential than its surgical products parent, it was quickly granted independence.

Creating a Horizontal Structure

Amoeba, reverse holding company, information partnership, joint venture, and spin-off—a rich variety of options for reshaping the new corporation. Despite their diversity, they all share a key characteristic. They emphasize the horizontal. They either allow for or mandate a corporate structure much wider than it is tall.

No single plan is appropriate for every company wanting to move its structure in this direction. Downsizing alone certainly will not work; frequently all it creates is an organization that looks like a warmed wedge of Swiss cheese. What a company needs to do to create a horizontally oriented structure depends on where it is starting from.

For some companies, the starting point will involve a *pulling together* of interrelated activities that may have strayed overtime. Siemens "discovered" that the employees who designed railway switches had no easy horizontal organizational linkage with those making electrical systems for trains. After pulling these and other railroad-related activities together in one division with a defined group of common customers, many ways to share and leverage capabilities and to market intelligence emerged. In less than four years, Siemens's sales almost doubled in what is frequently written off as a low-growth, mature industry.

Pulling together activities to achieve sharper customer focus is equally important in service industries. Swissair is using the routes in its schedule—through which its customers experience the airline—as the basis for creating its organizational clusters. As part of a revitalization effort, Sears, Roebuck & Company realized that most customers come to its stores to purchase from a specific department, not to scan the array of all Sears merchandise. But its organization structure was built around the store as its basic unit—a reflection of Sears' once successful strategy of emphasizing its own brands and its unique approach to customer service.

Sears changed this strategy by identifying seven of what it calls "power formats" (such as Brand Central, its store-within-the-store for consumer appliances and electronics). Each is a separate organization, pulled together from what were quasi-independent store operations and procurement groups. Each is responsible for its own buying, pricing, selling, and profitability. No longer will the apparel department hold a sale in an effort to maximize the store's profits by attracting busy shoppers who, it is hoped, will have their car serviced by Sears on the same visit. Nor will Sears be bound to keep each format in each store. Some formats, such as its Home Life furniture operation, have already been spun off into focused stores of their own.

Other businesses will give more attention to *splitting apart* activities or functions. Hewlett-Packard's profits rebounded and its number of new-product introductions soared when a single computer division became two: one selling minicomputers and workstations directly to large corporations, the other selling printers and personal computers through dealers to the mass market. Each requires different sales strategies; each now has its own sales force.

This idea can be applied either to an entire corporation or to one of its functions. Niagara Mohawk Power, a large upstate New York utility, abandoned its industry's historical pattern of tight vertical integration (the planar structure) and broke its operations into four entities, each responsible for its own growth and profit. One is focused on providing gas service to its customers, another to delivering electricity. A third unit generates electricity from traditional sources, and the fourth produces electricity from nuclear reactors.

Threatening competition from the Far East in the early 1980s forced the Illinois Tool Works to reshape its manufacturing approach. Compared to many Japanese factories, its facility in Elgin, Illinois, was best characterized as not "so much an assembly line as a loose confederation of city-states that periodically engaged in mutual commerce." Several advanced manufacturing techniques were applied to improve the situation, including the drastic change of isolating the equipment and the people who produced nine of the plant's high-volume components and setting them up in small, stand-alone operations in Wisconsin farmland. None of these plants has more than twenty-five employees; at each, a much stronger sense of identification of worker with product occurs than was ever possible in the centralized but internally balkanized Elgin facility.

Both Merck and USAA used the composite team as the basic building material to form structures based on splitting apart larger, more monolithic operations. USAA, a Texas-based insurance and financial services company, several decades ago eliminated the large functional groups handling insurance underwriting and servicing. Instead, five smaller organizations were created, each with all the specialists needed to handle all of a customer's needs. Each was assigned a fifth of USAA's customers, with each grouping containing a similar geographic and actuarial cross section of the entire customer pool. Then the five groups were put into competition with each other to provide motivation and to identify the company's next generation of management superstars. Employees who knew and cared about only their small segment of the company's operations quickly became insurance generalists, able to see how they could help all the pieces best fit together.

This splitting-apart technique works just as well outside the United States. In Italy, headquarters for multinational pharmaceutical giant Merck's research into viral diseases, lab operations have been subdivided into teams. Each focuses on specific diseases or promising chemical compounds. But the teams do not just discover something new and pass it on to someone else in Merck for testing, regulatory approvals, and selling. Each team stays with the product through the marketing phase, giving the researchers a stronger stake in their work's commercial success.

The Enterprise Unit

Business rearrangements such as these are moving toward the creation of a more horizontally oriented company, one that works faster across its structure than up and down. This form is the next stage in the evolution of the "strategic business unit" concept. To differentiate it from the old SBU, let's call it the *enterprise unit*.

Whereas the SBU's structure included all the activities necessary for it to function as a stand-alone entity, the enterprise unit performs only the activities most vital to its competitiveness, primarily those representing critical and cutting-edge capabilities. Other needed capabilities are purchased in the marketplace or shared with other enterprise units.

Whereas the SBU used the worker-and-boss pair as its basic organizational building block, the enterprise unit relies more on reinforced jobs and composite teams to get things done, in the manner of Merck and USAA. While SBUs, and the hierarchal superstructure above them, were full of part-time managers with fragmented responsibilities, enterprise units have few managers. But all managers are load-bearing. And while the SBU's implicit objective was to grow the business and increase the size of its organization as much as possible, the enterprise unit is more mindful of the advantages and disadvantages of scale. When growth happens, it is dealt with through the kind of corporate mitosis practiced by Cypress, Illinois Tool Works, and Johnson & Johnson.

SBUs are usually a reflection of the intersection of a corporation's products with the markets it serves. Organizing around these market segments provides better focus than can be obtained when the organization is based on specific products or the functions needed to produce them. The product-market matrix is a good way to plan when an industry is relatively mature and stably segmented, but it tends to produce organizational fossils when the rules of competition keep changing.

Instead, the enterprise unit's outputs are best defined as those meeting *common customer needs*, not just common customers. As these needs evolve, so do the enterprise units. Every member of an enterprise unit has what Paul Allaire, Xerox's chief executive, likes to call a direct line of sight to each customer. Small scale and sharp focus make this possible.

Organizing Around Processes, Not Functions

The most significant difference between SBUs and enterprise units is how jobs and teams are configured within the units. In most corporations, serious debate about organization structure is limited to the jobs on the top third of the organization chart. Bottom-up planning and the critical importance of the business's horizontal structure are either ignored or left to be resolved later in an uncoordinated manner. As a result, many so-called major organization overhauls are really just variations on some tired themes, especially the theme of functions as the best way to group whatever goes on in a business. This approach is prevalent even in many highly decentralized structures that pride themselves on divisional autonomy.

What from the top down might look like a great deal of freedom and flexibility is, from the bottom up, an undercoordinated, underleveraged patchwork of middle-management fiefdoms. The well-meaning basis for most of these enclaves is the seldom-questioned assumption that the function is the best unit to structure around: "Let's put the product designers in one department here, manufacturing over there, sales out on its own, and personnel and legal far enough away to keep out of everyone's hair. And then we'll let each use their best functional judgment about how to serve the corporation." While it is popular to talk about the necessity for plastic and planar structures, this basically skeletal model is still dominant throughout most corporations. Functional thinking—and the blinders that come with it—dominates the organizations of most of the world's companies. This, of course, leads to the wall building and corporate sclerosis that now have become so trendy to decry.

The streamlined flow charts emerging from process reengineering are attempts to deal with this excessive compartmentalization. But they remain weak half-steps unless their logic is transferred to the organization chart. (See Figure 8.) There is no point in resizing work along the horizontal lines of process flow if, in the end, it is only going to be awkwardly stuffed into a vertical, functional structure. Really managing a company by means of its key processes requires more than an overlay on functional fiefdoms. To do this we have to think about *creating orga-*

Figure 8. The reshaping process (2).

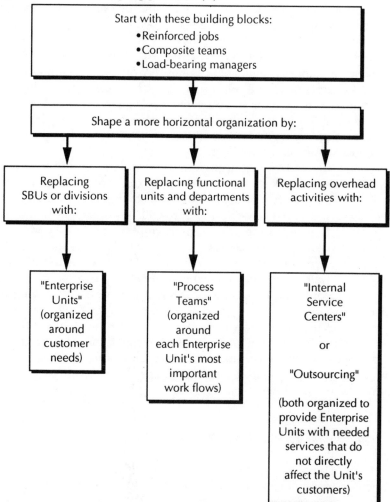

nization units for each key process that produces a result for the customer, instead of departments for each functional speciality. If the first level of the organization chart is inhabited by people in reinforced jobs or composite teams, the second tier is home to load-bearing managers in charge of the enterprise's most important business processes.

Lawrence Bossidy, Allied-Signal's chief executive, is a firm believer in this style of organization. He suggests that every enterprise unit has five or six basic processes and that they provide the best foundation on which to build a corporate structure. They are the engines that deliver a company's capabilities to its customers, and they are different for each enterprise. Top-down capability analysis is the key to identifying the processes worthy of driving the structure. For some companies, the list will include a seamless stream of activities that obtains and fulfills orders from customers. Others will want to include the cycle from product creation to market introduction, and some companies, such as Wal-Mart, may also want to stress a well-greased logistics machine or perhaps all the activities necessary to find, motivate, and retain loyal employees in time of increasing labor shortages.

A house divided against itself cannot stand—and neither can a company. Business processes cannot, despite the optimistic hopes of matrix organizers, flourish in a structure that is also subdivided along functional lines. Too much day-to-day effort will be consumed within the company sorting out these self-imposed conflicts to do a good job of continually improving the business processes and keeping them moving in the same directions as customers' needs. Planar and skeletal structures mix as well as oil and water; they can be only temporarily homogenized, and only if a lot of energy is spent continuously shaking the container that holds them. If processes are chosen as the basis for the second tier of the corporate structure, then most inhabitants of the existing functional groups will need new homes and their old departments will disappear from the organization chart. Functional walls will cease to be load-bearing, replaced by the managers who head each of the handful of key processes. New structures depend on new building materials.

Keeping Rein on the Business Processes

The shape of a company organized along the lines of enterprise units is distinctly horizontal (see Figure 9). Jobs are broad, not narrow. Self-direction is stressed over the establishment of tall management hierarchies, and businesses are organized around the lateral connections among processes, not the up-and-around-the-hierarchy direction provided by functional myopia.

What overall structure is best at containing all this high-speed activity? To whom will the leaders of the various enterprise units report? How will the corporation avoid losing the beneficial side of its functional expertise? What kind of oversight will maximize capability sharing and minimize the growth of bottom-up duplication of effort? From where will come the company's common aesthetic, its values? These are im-

Figure 9. Horizontal organization—the faster, broader approach.

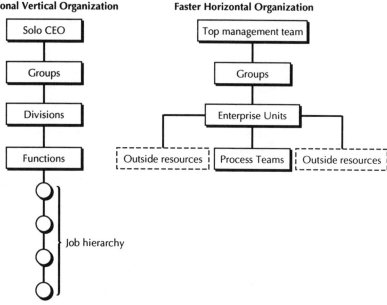

portant concerns. If they are not addressed, centrifugal forces will dominate as each hard-charging enterprise unit moves outward, following the call of its customers' most immediate needs.

Unfortunately, these are still open issues in the wake of many reorganizations. One multibillion-dollar company in the fast-growing information services industry took out two-page color advertisements in business periodicals around the world to announce the results of its dramatic restructuring. To cope with new competitors and to pave the way for major overseas expansion, many changes were made. Departments were resized, business processes were flow-charted and streamlined, and formerly independent units were collapsed into a megaorganization to cut redundancies and to allow capabilities to flow unimpeded by divisional walls. The company's overall head count shrank by many thousands, and, most dramatic of all, its newly reorganized headquarters was staffed by just under 100 employees (previously, this office had several thousand executives and managers, along with their staffs).

To symbolize all these "improvements," the advertisements featured a tough, rugged cowboy atop a fast-charging stallion. Their tone was highly self-congratulatory as they announced a complete corporate makeover.

Several years after the ads appeared, I was asked by an editor at *Fortune* to help with a story the magazine was researching on multibillion-dollar businesses that directed their operations with fewer than 100 headquarters employees. At that time, having 100 headquarters workers had become some sort of magical benchmark that signified successful reorganization, the leanest-shaped headquarters possible, and *Fortune* wanted the names of top companies that met this standard.

I suggested several, including manufacturing companies such as Dana and Hanson Industries, transportation giants Burlington Northern and CSX, and, of course, the well-known steel minimill innovator Nucor. To round out the list, I wanted to pass on the name of the proud information services company I had heard about several years before. But first, because my information was out of date, I checked back to get the latest head count at the top. I was expecting the downward trend to have continued, for the headquarters staff to be at seventy-five or possibly even fifty. After all, this company was a world-class bureaucracy-buster.

But the information headquarters passed on was surprising. At this point, there were more than 500 positions in this now bulging-at-the-seams headquarters, and this number was expected to continue increasing over the next few years! The quid pro quo for providing these discouraging data was a promise that the company's name would not be released to *Fortune,* a promise that, as a one-time consultant to this company, I felt compelled to keep. But I could not help wondering what had gone wrong.

PART THREE
RETHINK

Chapter 9
Make Each Level Count

Hierarchy will not completely disappear, but it can be tamed. Assign a specific time horizon to each level on the organization chart.

A fivefold increase in headquarters staffing in less than five years—hardly the mark of a successful, sustainable reorganization. Unfortunately Chapter 8's information services company is far from alone in experiencing a hockey stick-like staffing pattern. For streamlining to be other than just a temporary event between two ongoing periods of organization bloat, more needs to happen than head count reduction and work streamlining. Creating a properly shaped horizontal organization is vital, but it alone is not sufficient.

It is worth examining what went wrong at this boastful restructurer. What caused its 100-person, leanly shaped headquarters to regrow so large, so rapidly? One clue is in the titles of the jobs that were added during the rebound period: assistant vice-president of this, director of that. In addition, almost every senior officer managed to acquire one or two deputies or special assistants. Judging from job titles alone, possibly these 100 senior executives just got lonely. Or perhaps they had, over their careers, distanced themselves so far from doing direct work that they found they just needed some helpers. Whatever the reason, several new levels of management did emerge at this home office, just to provide oversight and direction to the company's operating units (most of whom already had another five layers of supervision in their own organizations).

The roots of this problem, of course, go well beyond loneliness or laziness (neither of which was a problem in this company). This restructurer did have a problem sustaining its hard-won gains, though, because it inadvertently created several organizational vacuums in the process of its reorganizing.

The first vacuum developed as management levels were cut and spans of control broadened. The old sources of tight supervision and control, dysfunctional as they once were, were no longer available to provide a sense of direction. Neither were rule books and procedure manuals. In the lean and mean mode of operation, less time was available to read and follow such guides, let alone write and update them. Another vacuum.

And what of the auditors and staff police department? These were among the first functions to go from headquarters when its size was cut to 100. The net result: Another serious vacuum was created.

Organizational vacuums, like vacuums in the physical world, are unstable. They need to be filled, and companies have two choices about how this will happen. The organization can revert to its old ways, especially when the economic pressures that prompted the initial changes are relaxed. This is what happened at the information services company. Alternatively, new tactics can be sought to provide direction and control—for which the need will not go away just because a business is reshaped.

Finding these new tactics requires *rethinking* many of the management practices that have become so common they are now usually taken for granted. This effort may be time-consuming and difficult, but it is necessary if organization change is to be sustainable.

Rethinking the Organization's Infrastructure

An architect's work requires more than site selection and structural design. A building also has an *infrastructure*, a complex and sometimes invisible web of systems that work together to make the building functional and livable. These include the mundane heating, electrical, plumbing, and air circulation systems, as well as the essential channels for people movement and telecommunication hookup.

Infrastructure is not just an add-on. The development of new technologies that provide efficient solar heating also required architects to consider a new set of factors when siting a building. Just as the invention of the elevator paved the way for today's concrete and steel skyscrapers, some new organizational concepts and technologies are needed to make horizontally oriented structures workable and vacuum-free.

This chapter and the three that follow describe the organizational infrastructure needed to make the new corporation work. Issues such as the hierarchy of reporting relations, the career structures they imply, and the middle managers who populate them are considered, along with ways to rethink control and coordination so that new learning, rather than resigned compliance, is produced.

Is Hierarchy All That Bad?

We like to say we are living in a posthierarchical business world, but rethinking sometimes requires reconsidering the value of some organizing practices that were once popular but now have fallen into disfavor. A surprise occurs when this is done: The posthierarchical corporation turns out to be one not completely without hierarchy. While the age of the corporate dinosaur may have passed and while the Egyptian pyramids no longer serve as role models for good organization structure, the need for reporting relationships and earmarked accountabilities has not yet completely disappeared. But their nature, and the rationale behind their layering, needs, in most companies, some serious rethinking.

The wave of global reorganizing that began in the 1980s has left many problems in its wake, especially regarding the role of the manager in the new corporation. Middle managers are popular targets for criticism, in large part because of their presence, in some companies, in multiple layers. An employee of a large computer maker, one long overdue for a major organizational overhaul, observed that his employer had a vast hierarchy of managers whose singular talent was that of career advancement. Other critics have been no less blunt. Two Harvard Business School professors who investigated the reasons behind the failure of many factory automation programs (such as computer-aided design, computer-aided manufacturing, robotics, and flexible manufacturing systems) concluded that, while these technologies show great promise, they are generally being installed into organizations too obsolete to make full use of them. Among the most dated aspects of these organizations, according to Robert Hayes and Ramchandran Jaikumar, is their tendency to staff production management positions with "specialized caretakers" who are more comfortable with relationships up and down the hierarchy than across it.

Some companies have found themselves in "damned if you do, damned if you don't" positions regarding middle management. When they eliminate excess layers and attempt employee empowerment programs, they are sometimes faced with an "I wasn't hired to be a manager" backlash. Often the remaining managers are implored to act more like leaders than managers, but they end up feeling unclear about exactly in what direction they are expected to lead.

In spite of these concerns, management jobs remain sought after. A study of U.S. college student attitudes conducted by Right Associates, career transition consultants, found that more than 80 percent of those with an interest in business expect to be managers or supervisors within five years of starting their careers. The conflicts caused by this strong demand for entry management jobs and the reality that such jobs are likely to be in short supply also will resonate through many corporate hierarchies as employees in mid-career cope with their own concerns about underpromotion and plateauing.

Just as it has become popular to deny the value of organization structure, critics often single out hierarchy as an unquestioned evil. But is it really?

Look closely at what was considered in the early 1980s as the model of corporations to come, the start-up airline People Express. This company, which has already vanished from the aviation industry, was a paragon of the "push authority far down the ranks" school of management. In fact, there were hardly any ranks at People Express. Every employee was designated a manager. But, as Robert Levering found in his research into what makes some companies especially good to work for, if everybody is a manager, then—from a political viewpoint—no one really is. Levering found a huge power vacuum between the executives at the top of People Express and everyone else who worked there. The lack of a viable middle management structure resulted in many ignored "mid-level" problems: People at the top were too busy; no one at the bottom had the necessary perspective or authority. The gap in the middle undoubtably contributed to the airline's demise.

The Psychological Fallout From Eliminating Hierarchies

Completely dismantling hierarchy may be poor politics, but it is even worse psychology. As hierarchy is reduced, anxiety frequently increases. And this increase is coped with in a number of dysfunctional ways. Some employees become increasingly rigid and bureaucratic, undermining the hoped-for flexibilities that were supposed to emerge from delayering. Others seem more prone to making mistakes and to having accidents, and some suffer from burnout as they try to carry out all their old responsibilities, in addition to providing the early warnings about emerging problems that their boss once gave.

Larry Hirschhorn, of the Wharton Center for Applied Research, studied what happens to workers who have had their responsibilities enlarged in the wake of management delayering. In the old order, supervisors and middle managers played two important roles. One was the traditional function of providing coordination and integration of work flows. This was relatively easy to hand off to the computer system or to delegate downward. The second key role, Hirschhorn observed, was less easy to give away or to automate. In that role, managers offered to their subordinates psychological protection against anxiety and fear of the unknown. This buffer effect is something that relationships with effective hierarchal superiors can also provide.

Facing risk and uncertainty is always hard. But it is usually easier when you know you are not alone. Strong ties with teammates and peers certainly help but can also lead to shared delusions or isolating camaraderie unless coupled with a sense of direction and linkage to where the rest of the company is going. For that, someone apart from the immediate work team is needed, someone who can help resolve the increase in tensions and conflict that close teamwork can generate. At People Express, Levering found to his great surprise, the biggest complaint of the airline's "employee self-managers" was they lacked a sense of management direction as the company grew and competition intensified. Ironically, these workers, selected for their ability to be self-motivated, wanted more direction and coordination, not less.

Abraham Zaleznik, one of the few Harvard Business School professors with psychoanalytic training, also confirms the psychological usefulness of hierarchy. He observes that detaching work from authority relations encourages irrational behavior. Some people become devious, whereas other focus more on *how* to do things than on the substance of *what* they are doing.

These problems are becoming increasingly common in many "empowerment" programs. Empowerment alone—without connection to a competitively significant task—can leave employees wondering just exactly what they are supposed to be doing so differently. One of Zaleznik's colleagues at Harvard, former PepsiCo president Andrall Pearson, calls empowerment "an idea in search of a place to happen." From where is this substance, these competitively significant tasks, supposed to come? Will they emerge out of the day-to-day flow of the horizontal organization, or is some superstructure still required to generate them? And if, as appears to be necessary, it is conceded some hierarchy is required, what should be the driving force behind its layering?

A Time-Based Superstructure

Time is one of the key performance measures of a process-driven horizontal organization. The key to competitive success in many markets is minimizing cycle time—how long an important business process takes from start to finish. The horizontal organization reduces cycle time through measures such as eliminating functional fiefdoms, broadening jobs, replacing SBUs with enterprise units, and organizing each of these units around the five or six processes that most drive its competitive advantage. The horizontal organization is a fast-moving place, a bundle of kinetic energy. It is working best when working fast.

Time is also a key factor driving how the superstructure above all this activity is configured. If the horizontal aspect of an organization represents the company's kinetic motion, then its vertical dimension symbolizes potential energy, its ability to maintain a measure of balance in the face of both today's and tomorrow's challenges. The quality of time most important here is its horizon, not its duration. *The vertical organization works best when oriented to the future.*

Time Frame and Organization Level

A hierarchy, when layered appropriately, allows several expanding time frames, or horizons, to be mapped on a company's structure. At the structure's lowest level, managers are concerned primarily with the events taking place within the cycle time of the business process they oversee. This may be as short as a day if they are managing Federal Express's overnight delivery business or as long as several years if they are responsible for one of the teams at Merck that stays with a new pharmaceutical from its discovery to its market introduction.

Most first-level managers, the people to whom team leaders or employees with reinforced jobs report, have time horizons of approximately *one year*. This is the time frame in which operational costs can be planned and controlled, changes in competitors' tactics observed and countered, and deviations from customer requirements spotted and corrected.

Above this level in the hierarchy are the managers of the various enterprise units the company has created. Most of their activities should produce results that will be readily apparent in a *two- to three-year* time frame. In this horizon, capital budgets are prepared, competitive strategies for the enterprise unit are developed, and new products are taken from idea to market entry.

Then, depending on a corporation's complexity and scope, a third stratum of managers might oversee a group of enterprise units. These cluster executives concentrate on their group's performance and growth over a *five-year* period and report to a top management group or a chief executive whose actions are geared to the promises and threats facing the corporation over the next *decade*.

These expanding time perspectives are directly related to the idea, presented in Chapter 3, that a company is really just a portfolio of capabilities. Some of these capabilities were classified as necessary to the current functioning of the company but not key to distinguishing it from its competitors. These were called core capabilities. Others were defined as more critical to the business's current success, and a few (called cutting-edge capabilities) we said were valuable primarily for their future promise.

Over a five-year time period, some critical capabilities may lose their power to drive competitive success and become part of the business's core. Their place may be taken by what were cutting-edge competences that have become the new basis for competitive differentiation.

Group or cluster executives should spend a considerable amount of time making sure multiyear transitions like this happen smoothly. They should also ensure the capabilities of each enterprise unit are easily available to others who can make good use of them. In addition, they should monitor shifts in customer needs and keep alert to new markets that these capabilities can serve.

The ten-year-out perspective of the chief executive or the senior management team has its own way to add value, again keyed to the kinds of events that may take a decade to unfold. This level factors into the company's decision making the implications of long-term political, social, and demographic change, as well as shifts in the underlying structures of the industries in which the corporation participates.

These time periods are illustrative (see Figure 10), not set in concrete. They need to be uniquely specified for each company. What cannot vary, though, are their broadening as one ascends the hierarchy, and their discrete nature. Each level needs to be self-contained. Levels that overlap or that come close to overlapping in future orientation are good clues that the vertical structure has too many resting places.

How Many Layers of Hierarchy Are Enough?

These time horizons are similar to those found by London-based organization researcher Elliott Jaques in over forty years of investigation into what makes for an effective organization structure. Jaques has long advocated adding a measure of rationality to organization hierarchy by grouping work assignments by the length of time they require to complete. His research, rooted in cognitive psychology, provides a useful way to think about the maximum number of levels an organization structure should have.

Figure 10. Match each level of the hierarchy with a time span.

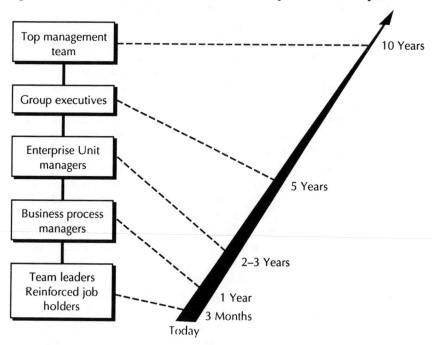

Jaques maintains that seven hierarchal layers are sufficient, and frequently more than sufficient, for all but the world's very largest corporations. Making changes in the way work and jobs are structured at the bottom of the hierarchy can allow for even fewer levels, such as the maximum of four or five that this book advocates. Jaques's research identifies organization layers at the one-day and three-month cutoffs. The time horizons these reflect, though, are those contained in what is called here the "horizontal organization." They need to be dealt with through reinforced jobs and composite teams, not through additional vertical superstructure.

For example, consider Asea Brown Boveri, Ltd. (ABB), a $25 billion global leader in electrical equipment manufacturing. Its management structure never allows more than five people to be between the shop floor and the chief executive. How many employees can such a thin structure contain? ABB employs almost a quarter of a million people! They are kept coordinated and on track by ABB's appropriate use of scale in its horizontal organization. ABB has more than 4,000 individual enterprise units, but each averages only 50 employees. A lean superstructure requires the solid foundation of a well-designed horizontal organization.

Jaques sees these superstructure levels as fixed strata. They are driven by the escalating degrees of difficulty in processing information and in making decisions that occur as an executive's time horizon broadens. Moving from one stratum to another is analogous to what chemists call changes of state: the transformations that occur when ice changes to water and water to steam at certain fixed temperatures. Jaques observes that certain time frames serve as similar barriers; crossing them requires a quantum difference in managerial capacity. While he believes these time-defined strata are an indication of some universal truth about human nature, they can also be accepted as a reflection of the common-sense hope expressed by many employees immersed in their company's day-to-day activities that "someone up there" has time to worry about the business's future.

Today's Agenda Drives Tomorrow's Results

Having managers and executives spend ever increasing amounts of time on longer-term issues does not mean that the time is necessarily spent in planning meetings, closeted with a few trusted advisors, or in solitary introspection. These are not necessarily the best ways to give future focus to a job. Nor does it mean that all their time will be spent on activities dictated by the time frame ascribed to the management level they occupy. When an immediate business-threatening crisis occurs, it will not be ignored just because an executive occupies a slot with a five- or ten-year horizon. But, in the course of, say, a year, the executive's *agenda* should reflect time spent on matters in sync with what is expected at his or her level.

Manager's agendas, at all levels, are lived out in the day-to-day world, filled with many mundane and unplanned activities. The trick in keeping focused on a future time frame is to ensure that the manager's particular horizon is clearly reflected in how this time is spent, who is seen, what is discussed, what questions are asked, what stories are told, and which performance indicators are most closely watched.

Changes like this, clearly mapping the future on the management structure, are vital if the new corporation is to have an appropriate rationality behind its hierarchy, one that links each level with a time frame of greatest relevance to the part of the company being directed and that keeps the levels from having overlapping horizons. Unfortunately, today, few such structures are oriented this way in practice. Levels are designated because of the dictates of personnel classifications or pay systems, the expansive logic of both tending to breed many more layers than are needed to run the business. Extra layers reflect the dictates of functional control, political accommodations, and strategies once successful but now irrelevant. They also often serve as memorials to past mistakes.

Several years ago a chemical company suffered a major disaster when a plant exploded, killing several employees and causing serious public concern about the company's safety practices. Later, its president insisted the problem was caused by execessive decentralization and pulled responsibility for all the manufacturing facilities away from the executives who planned and sold the plant's products. A separate manufacturing hierarchy, reporting directly to the president, was created, adding two levels to the company's structure. While this seemed to allow for special attention to the needs of these plants, it also made it very difficult for the executives dependent on the plant's outputs to have much direct influence over issues of prime concern to their customers, such as product quality and delivery time. Eventually, this company lost a sizable share of its market to more customer-oriented competitors.

Plant safety concerns are vitally important in this and many other industries. But assuming that the best solution to such concerns is the creation of extra hierarchy and refunctionalization is as dangerous to the business's health as it is to the workers'. Other companies have had better results handling similar safety problems through a combination of increased training and better use of the existing management structure. These companies ensure that concern for sales and production is matched with concern for employee safety at the level of the structure where these concerns are most relevant: the lower levels of the hierarchy where managers appropriately focus on the day-to-day. The creation of extra management level dilutes, not increases, this accountability.

Reflecting increasing time horizons on the vertical structure is one of the surest ways for each level to add some discrete value to the work done by those below. Perhaps Jaques's most important observation about managers is that they need to be held accountable for both the *results* of their subordinates and for *their contribution to adding to these results*. A manager's results have to be more than just the arithmetic sum of what subordinates produce. The major problem with excessive management layers is that managers are too close in time frame to the work of their subordinates. As a result, they cannot delegate "complete tasks." If they do, what will be left for them to do? The result is what are often called "straw bosses" and demotivated subordinates, problems commonly found in studies of organization structure around the world, as well as in the research done by General Electric on fragmented management jobs.

In some misstructured hierarchies, an even more dangerous problem emerges. It is one of *inversion:* work structured so that most of the attention to the business's future comes from those on the lower rungs of the hierarchy. Maybe this is to be expected if the senior managers are busy micromanaging their subordinates, who (finding their bosses doing their jobs) are just looking for some way to make a contribution. While long-range issues need to be every employee's concern if a business is to stay healthy, accountability for them cannot be expected to rest with those whose scope and power are mismatched with the challenges the issues pose.

Lack of clearly demarcated time horizons for each level of the vertical organization is a problem plaguing many corporations, and one well worth some serious rethinking. But another difficulty will be even more problematic in the future. It is the assumption that everyone occupying a place on the hierarchy must be a manager.

Chapter 10

Fuse Knowledge to Power

Establish a path for professional career advancement. Make it possible to have influence without being a manager.

Architects are concerned with flows. When designing a building, their paramount considerations are how occupants will move in it and how light and air will circulate around it. Equally important for organizational architects is how information, know-how, decisions, and careers will flow in the structure being shaped.

When the work of the corporation was primarily the organizing of manual labor, markets were local and slow to change, and the knowledge base upon which competitive success depended was stable, a unitary hierarchy of manager atop manager made a lot of sense. The information needed to run the business was limited and could be easily channeled in one upward or downward flow. Workers did the work, and managers did the thinking.

But this is a reality that has disappeared from most industries. Markets are dimensioned globally, rules change faster than some competitors can master them, and brainpower counts for much more than brawn. Most organizations, though, remain keyed to the old realities. Few hierarchies have even kept up with the need to build in change by linking each of their limited number of levels with the time horizons of greatest importance to the company. Wall Street is blamed for American businesses' preoccupation with the short term, when the problem is just as much a result of inadequate organization structures.

A more serious problem, though, is the lack of rethinking about how a business needs to organize its intellectual capital, its knowledge workers. It is ironic, and wasteful, that while "knowledge workers" (technical professionals and other holders of college and graduate degrees) are making up an increasing proportion of the work force in many industries, the organization structures in which they work remain more the products of the Industrial Revolution than of the information age.

Knowledge, especially that which can affect the company's future competitiveness, used to be confined to the research and development lab or to the strategic planning department. Now, as information systems-driven service industries assume a larger share of many economies, knowledge about the capabilities that provide competitive advantage is much more widely dispersed than was ever necessary in traditional manufacturing companies. No single information channel can contain it all. And even traditional product makers are changing. Fewer manufacturing jobs are directly involved in making something; more are concerned with planning what to make, how to make it, and how to keep customers happy after the product has been purchased. As Saab found in its robot-filled plant in Trollhattan, the intellectual demands on front-line workers have increased tremendously. The narrowly skilled assembly job has been replaced by the more knowledge-intensive position of the factory automation technician.

Requirements for more intellectual value added have escalated up many organization hierarchies. Networked data bases, expert systems, and an almost never-ending flow of new personal computer software have significantly expanded the scope and the nature of the contribution possible from many mid-level employees. This is not an unmitigated blessing, though. It has also seriously polluted the management role in many companies, making many into high-level doers instead of managers, increasing the role's fragmentation, and making it brittle rather than strong and load-bearing.

This situation will only worsen as economic pressures lead to increased management delayering. Companies with eight to ten tiers of management will find it necessary to organize around four or five. The number of subordinates per manager will have to sharply increase. Middle managers will find themselves with less and less time to master these new white-collar productivity enchancers and to make the intellectual contribution their businesses increasingly need.

How have industries that have been traditionally knowledge-oriented organized themselves? Are lessons about the shape of the industrial hierarchy of the future available from the structures used by today's think tanks, consulting firms, universities, and hospitals? Are any practices that have worked well for organizations that employ primarily professionals, such as accountants, architects, and lawyers, relevant to other businesses whose future is increasingly dependent on how they manage the carriers of their intellectual capital?

Advancement in a Professional Service Firm—An Example

Arthur D. Little, Inc., a worldwide consulting and research organization, is essentially in the business of selling the time of its professional staff. It makes money only when consultants are busy helping clients. Too much management overhead quickly destabilizes any consulting firm's economics. Since it has remained in business for more than 100 years, significantly longer than other firms in its industry, it may be worth examining how Arthur D. Little manages a stable of knowledge workers. Consider the career progression of one of its more successful professionals.

Let's call him Jacques Decartes. A Swiss, he received an M.B.A. from Harvard Business School twenty years ago. After graduation, he was hired to work as an Arthur D. Little management consultant in Brussels. Arthur D. Little's operation in Belgium was small at that time, so Decartes reported directly to the Brussels office manager.

Many years later I had dinner with Decartes. We discussed our careers, and I observed he still reported to the head of the Brussels operation. No movement up the hierarchy in twenty years! How did he maintain a sense of dignity at Harvard Business School reunions, where his classmates boasted of their senior vice-presidencies and divisional managing directorships?

Actually, he had no trouble holding his own with them. He holds an officer's title at Arthur D. Little. He leads consulting teams that directly serve the chief executives of some of Europe's most distinguished corporations (after he personally convinces them to hire Arthur D. Little). He is a leader of the company's technology and innovation practice in Europe and a codirector of its worldwide strategic planning business.

Decartes has a long history of developing or championing consulting products that bring considerable revenues to Arthur D. Little. For this, and for his accomplishments selling them, his total compensation can exceed that of his hierarchical superior. His professional reputation is not confined to his clients and colleagues; Decartes also frequently lectures at several leading European business schools. In recognition of his reputation, the company allowed him to adjust his schedule to serve as an adjunct faculty member at a business school.

Whereas earlier in his career he personally helped recruit and train new graduates, he is now more concerned with helping define the criteria by which they are selected and with overseeing the development of their training curricula. He used to serve as a sponsor to help some of the most promising recruits learn the ropes at Arthur D. Little; now he spends more time mentoring mid-level consultants with the potential to manage offices or lead practices.

The company has not accommodated these mentoring and external teaching activities merely to retain his services and keep him motivated. Decartes is a full member of what Arthur D. Little calls its European Directorate, a council consisting of the managers and the senior professionals (like Decartes) from each of its European offices. This group, by consensus, makes decisions or recommendations to the parent company about issues such as new offices to open, new products to develop, and new services to offer. It also monitors the financial performance of the business in Europe, considering both geographic office results and the success or failure of services and practices that cut across the offices. Competitive intelligence is pooled among its members and cross-Europe marketing initiatives planned.

Membership in this group firmly plugs Decartes—and the intellectual capital he carries—into the company's power structure. His ideas, and votes, carry the same weight as those of office managers. Though most of these managers supervise several dozen employees, Decartes oversees only a portion of his secretary's time.

Developing the Careers of Individual Contributors

It is becoming more accepted that senior professional contributors like Decartes will be vital to the knowledge-based new corporation. But from where will they come? What stages do they need to successfully pass through before reaching the highest levels of influence in their companies? How can knowledge about these developmental stages help plan a dual hierarchy? Fortunately, it is not necessary to reinvent the wheel to answer these questions. Two professors from Brigham Young University, Gene Dalton and Paul Thompson, have done much of the needed conceptualizing. Their many years of research about what makes for successful careers in an organization have yielded a number of starting points for the creation of a professional track for advancement.

Dalton and Thompson find four distinct stages in the careers of individual contributors who rise to the senior ranks of their organizations (see Figure 11). Each stage differs in the responsibilities considered most appropriate, the relationships considered most critical, and the psychological adjustments required. As with most developmental progressions, if one stage is skipped over or is not successfully handled, it is likely that related performance problems will emerge in succeeding ones.

Figure 11. The four phases of a professional's corporate career.

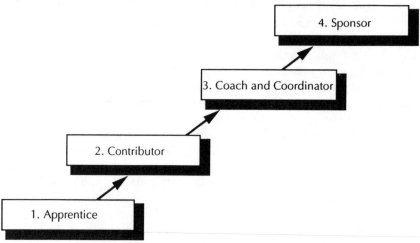

In the following discussion of Dalton and Thompson's four phases, I have restated and expanded their descriptions to make them as helpful as possible for a professional career track.

Phase 1: Apprentice

This entry career stage is the one at which acceptance into the company is earned. Newcomers become socialized and learn how to be good subordinates. Though it is often seen as belittling, knowing how to accept the dependencies that come with apprenticeship is something that will pay off just as much in later career stages as it does here. Even the chief executive has critical dependencies that need to be managed—and the price for not handling these well is highlighted in the increasing number of CEOs and other senior executives who are losing their jobs. It is too late to learn this skill at the peak of a career; it needs to be at the top of the apprentice's agenda.

The role of apprentice has changed little since the days of the guild system of medieval Europe. But its requirements have become increasingly difficult for beginning professionals to accept after they have spent several years in elite M.B.A. or other difficult graduate programs. Realistic pre-employment previews of this phase, its rationale, and the possibilities that will follow it are keys to successful passage through it.

Phase 2: Contributor

Most of a company's professional contributors are found at this stage of development. They have settled down to make their mark, usually by applying themselves diligently to a problem or to a technical specialty of immediate concern to the business. Unlike apprentices, who are expected to serve as competent helpers while learning the ropes, Phase 2 professionals assume responsibilities for independently carrying out definable projects. Their work, as with all reinforced jobs, has a clear beginning and an end to it, along with prespecified outcomes.

The trick here, for those who want to advance along the professional track, is to choose a content area or set of specialized skills that can be applied in many places and to many problems of the company.

This is a phase that can go wrong in two diametrically opposed ways. Some independent contributors become too narrowly specialized, possibly to a degree beyond the economic use of their employer. Others err by never developing any single, solid competence; they are too impatient to move into management.

While this is the point at which many professional careers have shifted to management roles, the new corporation's leaner superstructure and its greater emphasis on self-management will offer fewer openings on the managerial advancement track. The positive aspect of this limitation is that it allows a better chance for knowledge workers to lay a solid foundation for their future professional efforts.

Many solo contributors remain here; unfortunately, their jobs may be threatened if the capability they most support ceases to be important to their business's competitiveness. This stage is also as far as many traditional technical career ladders reach. This is the point where an employee is most likely to lose himself or herself in work, to become an elite master craftperson. The dangers of facing limited further advancement, if this choice is made, are offset for some by the sheer joy that comes from doing something they really love—not necessarily a bad trade-off. Just because a corporation has mapped out a hierarchy does not mean that everyone needs to climb it.

Phase 1 and Phase 2 professionals tend to work within the horizontal organization, assigned to one of the five or six key process groups that have replaced the traditional functional departments. These assignments alone provide them with a much broader view of the business than would have ever been possible in more isolated units composed of their professional peers. Rotations among several process groups or from one enterprise unit to another can also prepare some of these seasoned individual contributors for movement to the lean, vertical super-structure.

Phase 3: Coach and Coordinator

Fortunately for the new corporation's staffing needs, intrinsic rewards are not sufficient for everyone. For some employees, the congruence they find between their values and what the company stands for is stronger than the tug of their professional speciality.

For these workers, advancement to the third stage is possible. In it, as the contributors' responsibilities extend over a longer time horizon, they will also take on increased responsibilities for others. Earlier, they were responsible only for the quality of the assistance they provided or for their own individual work product. In Phase 3, they become more the proverbial "person in the middle." They are tugged in many directions by their hierarchal manager, their professional track peers, and their independent contributor colleagues at more senior levels. They do not have direct subordinates but may have assistants (either apprentices or individual contributors) to help as needed. (To ensure this setup does not build up an organization-within-the-organization, these assignments extend only for the life of whatever particular project the Phase 3 contributor is heading at that time.)

Phase 3 employees provide supervision—but project supervision, not oversight and management responsibility for an organization unit. Their work often falls within the accountability of someone on the management hierarchy; one project may cross the turf of several managers, creating additional relationships that must be skillfully balanced.

They are expected to serve as mentors to guide the development of those at the apprentice and the early independent contributor stages. These relationships need to be dynamic; Phase 3 professionals must receive recognition and incentive for the number of their protégés who graduate from one phase to another, not for how many assistants they collect.

This phase provides many opportunities to broaden the ways contributions are made. Individual contributors are expected to generate fertile, creative ideas that become—via the management structure—the work of others. For this to happen, it is essential for Phase 3 incumbents to learn how to sell ideas internally. They thus become key cross-links in the vertical hierarchy.

Phase 3 individual contributors have also been around the company long enough for something to have happened to the capabilities, customers, or markets to whose development they contributed. These may have died off or escalated in importance; either way, the Phase 3 professional will have learned the critical importance of adaptability.

Professionals in Phase 3 start, if they have not already done so, working closely with people outside the company, possibly via a second tour of duty assigned to a key supplier's or customer's facility. In Phase 3 the professional is expected to take on more responsibility for maintaining the relationship, rather than just performing solid work.

For many people, functioning well with these responsibilities, especially in a dynamic and growing company, can provide a career's worth of satisfaction. Some, though, may have additional ways to contribute to the business that make them candidates for further advancement.

Phase 4: Sponsor

Contributors at the Phase 4 level are in positions where they influence the entire corporation, or significant parts of it. These intellectual leaders work as partners with the leaders in the upper management hierarchy to set the direction of the enterprise, as Jacques Decartes does through his position in Arthur D. Little's directorate team. Decartes is very much an influential idea entrepreneur.

At times this power may be represented in money. There is no reason why a company's budget allocation process must allocate funds only to managers. Often sizable development budgets are put in the hands of Phase 4 professionals, along with a role in the allocation and oversight of funds apportioned to managers throughout the business.

A key way Phase 4 people influence the company's future, Dalton and Thompson have observed, is through their decisions about who should fill key job vacancies and what career paths other high-potential employees should follow. They are less concerned with getting newcomers started; that is the job of those in Phase 3. Rather, they assess the promise of Phase 2, incumbents to someday fill Phase 4 slots and provide these future stars with counsel, grooming, and chances at challenging assignments.

Their sponsorship of people and ideas is broader than mentoring. It is more of a political process, one aimed at helping bring about long-term change. They are among the organizational architects, creators of systems that bring about future results. Comfortable exercising power and forming political alliances, they take strong positions on issues without creating permanent enemies. The word "power" is not usually used when talking about knowledge workers, but it must be if their ideas and know-how are to be put to use. Having the right visions about where a market is headed is useless unless that knowledge is acted upon. Good Phase 4 contributors have in their heads a map of the future; the best of them also have the ability to encourage the company to substitute this map for that currently being followed.

More ideas supported by professionals in Phase 4 of their careers see the light of day than do those advanced by employees on lesser levels, because Phase 4 professionals are more firmly wired into the business's power structure. But their job is not to originate all these ideas. Instead, their responsibility is more to maintain a network across the company that stimulates, sorts, and selects from the best thinking available. Just as a glass wall brings light into a building, Phase 4 contributors are gateways for fresh insights about the business.

Frequently, their network extends well beyond the company. Many occupy key outside roles. They are active in industry, as well as professional associations, and serve on advisory committees and high-level civic projects. The most senior may join commissions to recommend improvements to national competitiveness or educational reform—posts too often given to chief executives who seldom have adequate time to bring their company's best ideas to these forums. Accepting assignments on boards of directors of key suppliers is another useful way Phase 4 talent can benefit the company.

These are people easily able to act *now* on ways that will pay off in the *future*. As Dalton and Thompson say, they "must learn to think about the organization as a whole and act in terms of that framework. They must learn to think about the needs of the organization beyond the time period during which they will personally be affected."

A Professional Track, Not a Track for Professionals

The parallel hierarchy in which nonmanagerial careers can develop is called a professional track, mainly to differentiate it from the narrower idea of the "technical" ladder. The word "professional" is used here to encompass all individual contributing knowledge workers, not just members of a select group in traditional professions.

Ironically, this hierarchy is frequently not the best way to structure the participation in the work of a company of relatively self-contained professionals, such as lawyers, physicians, technologists with strong academic learnings, and even behavioral scientists and organization development experts. Using the skills of people in fields such as these can often best be accomplished by treating them as consultants or contractors, structurally reinforcing their independence ⁀om the corporation (a key element of the value they add).

Members of many traditional professions argue their work deserves a measure of autonomy from the corporation because it is self-regulating. Self-regulation develops when their role has become institutionalized in society and is associated with:

- A defined knowledge base and a series of routines specifying when to apply what portion of it
- Some formal mechanism for regulating entry to the profession through an accreditation or certification process
- A standard of ethics or code of conduct and the existence of an external body to enforce them
- A professional culture that stresses a duty to use the profession to better society—a sense of mission or calling

Characteristics like these distinguish professions from other vocations. They are useful qualities, but they can also pose problems for some corporations. To the extent that they build a wall between professionals and others in a company, they can be counterproductive. Many professionals, though, are comfortable with this wall; its existence is incorporated into their routines of practice. Professionals tend to have clients or patients they serve, rather than teammates and colleagues. Traditional professionalism often leads to the creation of hierarchies of expertise, which, observes Abraham Zaleznik, "tend to fragment rather than bond people's relationships."

This sense of apartness had led professionals to play ambivalent roles in many organizations. Mutual suspicions and concerns about trust abound between them and their managers. Some professionals are seen as being much more concerned with their standing in their field than with their position in the company. Resentments form as some outside the professional's field see the person trying to achieve a disproportionate degree of autonomy by hiding behind a professional mystique.

These problems, once just minor annoyances, will become much more troublesome as the proportion of knowledge workers and employees with at least quasi-professional leanings increase in corporate work forces. Such workers' know-how cannot be purchased exclusively on the open market. But the difficulties associated with internalizing it can quickly torpedo the success of a parallel hierarchy if they are not taken into account as the new structure is implemented.

Avoiding these difficulties requires that a bargain be struck between the corporation and its knowledge workers. The company must recruit knowledge workers who find it attractive to give up a measure of their professional autonomy in exchange for a mechanism that ensures they have more influence over the direction of the business. Providing that mechanism is a key function of the professional track that reaches to the company's most senior management levels. Companies will also have to apply some creativity to make the rewards and recognition provided internally at least as compelling as those provided by the outside profession. Microsoft does this by designating promotion to one level of computer programmer as equivalent to making partner in a law firm. A big ceremony, with attendant hoopla in and outside the company, is provided for those reaching this stage. The objective is to have the employee's tie to the company become slightly stronger than the tie to the field or discipline. A key to achieving this is the provision of incentives that encourage and reward interdisciplinary thinking and a willingness to change one's perspective, not just hunker down in it.

Examples of the Professional Track in Practice

While few companies have fully developed systems that allow nonmanagers to play a significant part in corporate decision making, steps in this direction are becoming more common. Kodak has used senior individual contributors to help fill in the "white space" between product lines. Corning Glass Works has redesigned jobs for its older managers so that they can specialize in adapting existing products to meet emerging customer needs, rather than just focusing on the narrowing competition for senior executive positions. Both 3M and Ford have broadened their technical advancement ladders to include manufacturing and sales professionals.

A fast-food operator created a position called "senior technical advisor" and gave it status equivalent to that of its vice-president for operations. The advisor's role: to serve as a high-level troubleshooter to work one-on-one with franchisees. This job is given to some of the company's best field-oriented talent, people who might otherwise wilt on the vine if moved to headquarters.

This is not an idea limited only to the United States. One of the most innovatively organized companies anywhere, Brazil's Semco S.A., pays its professionals according to their contributions, rather than on the basis of their location in its minimally layered management hierarchy. It is common for Semco's "associates" to earn considerably higher salaries than their managers or even senior executives.

Practices like this will become more common as companies worldwide become aware of how dependent their future competitiveness is upon the creation of structures to accommodate the contributions of their knowledge workers. Their recruiting literature will declare, "You don't have to become a manager to get ahead here." In a business world where, increasingly, knowledge and information equate with power, those who possess these attributes need to join those who occupy the corporation's most powerful positions.

Chapter 11

Provide Two Paths
to the Top

*Ensure that the professional hierarchy extends as
far as the managerial one. Redefine the role of the
middle manager.*

For a parallel hierarchy to add the most value, it must extend all the way
to the top of the superstructure. *An inability to find productive roles for
senior individual contributors at the upper end of the hierarchy is a clear signal
that the dual path idea is not right for your company.* An increasing number
of companies are finding this not to be a problem.

The Parallel Hierarchy in Action

A clean, unobtrusive functional look is the hallmark of consumer products designed by Braun, the German maker of small appliances. This
spare appearance was created by Dieter Rams, the company's chief designer. It sets Braun's products apart and is one of the company's most
critical capabilities. Its importance to the company's competitiveness is
reflected by Rams's place in the corporate hierarchy; he reports directly
to the company's chairman, not through a marketing or engineering department. When Braun was purchased by Gillette, Rams was also given
direct access to the U.S. parent's chief executive. Gillette is a shrewd
acquirer; it made sure it managed Braun so as not to kill off the goose
that helped lay the golden eggs that made the company so worth buying
in the first place.

Here's a second example. During the late 1960s, the technology-
based conglomerate TRW, Inc., was run by a three-person top team. One
member was the chairman and chief executive. A second was the presi-

dent and long-in-advance designated heir apparent to the CEO's spot. The close-knit team's third member was Simon Ramo, officially designated the corporation's vice-chairman.

Ramo had no direct operating responsibilities; he served as the technology eyes and ears of TRW. Earlier in his career, when TRW was still just a metal-bending parts maker, he had been sent from the company's Cleveland corporate headquarters to California. His mission: to create a new division for TRW, one that would be based on electronics and systems engineering technologies. Several years later, his task completed, he returned to headquarters to serve as a technological entrepreneur role model for other rising executives. His example encouraged others to start up new businesses, such as TRW's now vast consumer credit reporting service, which sprang from the systems management capabilities Ramo helped nourish. And his willingness to be outspoken about broad public issues affecting the company and society in general helped pave the way for senior professionals such as Pat Choate, TRW's former vice-president for public policy, to be strong advocates for massive job retraining programs as essential to the future competitiveness of the United States.

Like Arthur D. Little's Jacques Decartes (see Chapter 10), Ramo also maintained a part-time academic affiliation, in his case a research associateship at California Institute of Technology. Unlike many professionals in large corporations, Ramo's interests broadened as his career advanced. Once the chief scientist for the United States' intercontinental ballistic missile program, he later applied the systems thinking pioneered there to developing fresh solutions to social problems. Before retiring from TRW, he reflected on his experiences managing the technological development of a $1 billion corporation and put in writing many of the key lessons he learned to serve as a guide to TRW's emerging generations of technology entrepreneurs.

Ramo's books and corporate title helped provide widespread recognition for his accomplishments. The "R" in his company's name, TRW, stands for Ramo. This is an honor received by neither the president nor the chairman with whom he shared the top management role in the 1960s.

A third example of the professional hierarchy at work is Microsoft. Managing competitive capabilities has gotten more complicated since the 1960s. Microsoft has not found any one individual to serve as its Simon Ramo, so it has appointed seven people to fill his role as seer and innovator. Called Microsoft's "architects," the seven people serve as a panel of technical high priests to advise chief executive Bill Gates on matters such as emerging technologies and overall software development strategy.

One of the group's members, Jeff Harbors, is already independently wealthy from his awards of stock options, granted during Microsoft's early days. But he stays on board because he sees the panel as a way he can still significantly contribute to the company's future. Gates, Microsoft's founder, has spent his entire career there. Unpolluted by experiences in more rigid, unitary corporate hierarchies, he modeled Microsoft's advancement structure after that of an organization he had some personal acquaintance with—a law firm. (Gates's father is a prominent Seattle attorney.)

Creating Structures That Link Power and Knowledge

Some Phase 4 contributors, like Ramo, are actual business entrepreneurs. Others, such as Dieter Rams, are high-level keepers of the corporate conscience; Braun's appliances all have a consistency behind their design because Rams has the power to veto any proposed products that deviate from the established norms.

This influence is not exercised in a vacuum, though. When power is granted to anyone in a company, it is to advance the needs of the business, not the personal interests of the power holder. Phase 4 contributors must be among the strongest keepers of the company's ethics. They must also avoid the other common trap facing those with a grant of power: the tendency to use it only to stop things from happening. Rams has earned his veto right because the products he has championed have been so successful in the marketplace.

In the future it may be possible to find senior positions, now part of the management hierarchy, that have been moved to the professional path. Allied-Signal's Lawrence Bossidy envisions the twenty-first-century corporation as still having a chief financial officer reporting to the chief executive, but without the traditional army of controllers, auditors, and accountants who now report to the chief financial officer. Instead, these staff positions will be based in the enterprise units and central service centers that will cluster in the company's horizontal organization. This pattern may well be repeated for the chiefs of other functional specialities, especially human resources, information systems, and research and development.

Organizations that acquire early experience in ways to link knowledge with power will be several steps ahead of their rivals as knowledge-based competition comes to dominate many industries. They will be companies that realize that career paths are more than just tools to maintain employee morale.

Corporate superstructures must be rethought so they reflect the new reality that *power needs to be expressed via knowledge and experience as well as through managerial authority*. Both kinds of leadership are crucial; a key challenge for the vertical organization is to keep them in balance. This idea has always been true to some extent; now its acceptance is becoming mandatory. Hospitals could not serve sick patients without the dual governance provided by a medical hierarchy and the separate administrative one. Nor do many universities educate students using faculty members who will admit to anything but an indirect and loose reporting relationship with the school's president and administrative hierarchy.

For most of its history while an independent company, the publisher Time, Inc., prided itself on its separation of "church" from "state." "Church," the editorial side of the business, reported through its editor in chief directly to the company's board. The publishing portion of the company ("state"), concerned with more mundane matters like advertising revenues and production expenses, had a parallel hierarchy that did not include the oversight of the editorial departments, as was the common practice in the rest of the more unitary publishing industry. This power-sharing arrangement was intended to give editors freedom to cover and analyze news stories without interference from the company's advertisers or financial managers. In the long run, it was hoped, this practice would help attract star journalists whose writing would increase *Time* magazine's value to its readers, ultimately making it a more attractive vehicle for advertisers.

At *Business Week*, published by a competitor of *Time*, a similar practice was applied on a smaller scale. The position of senior writer was created to provide an opportunity for high performers whose talents would be underused if they advanced to the traditional next step of department manager or editor. This is not a resting place for poor performers; senior writers include John Byrne, author of several business books and former editor of the magazine's Management Department. It is also a good home for Byrne's entrepreneurial inclinations; he helped originate the magazine's annual rankings of graduate business school programs, an activity that might otherwise fall between the cracks on the publication's organization chart.

The operating practices of many Japanese companies also reflect an awareness that relationships and practical knowledge can be just as important as managerial expertise. In each work location, senior executives operate through both the official management hierarchy and an unofficial de facto hierarchy. Consultations with the de facto leaders, who have emerged through a combination of accumulated experience, technical knowledge, and ability to command the personal respect of the other workers, are often held before decisions are announced through the official channels. These private discussions, called *nemawashi*, are especially important when business conditions worsen or significant changes in operating practices need to be made. By laying the structural groundwork, they make possible much of the consensus and harmony in Japanese workplaces that is commonly overattributed to national cultural values.

Broadening Traditional Technical Ladders

The idea of parallel hierarchies has been most commonly expressed through the dual career ladders offered by some technology-oriented companies. Aware that many good engineers and scientists find management work an anathema, these companies have provided a sequence of jobs, increasing in pay, title, and responsibility, that allows their technical staffs to advance without taking on any traditional supervisory or management responsibilities. The system that 3M put in place several decades ago to accomplish this is one of the best developed and the most effective. Without it, 3M's ubiquitous yellow notepad product, Post-it, might never have been created. Post-it's developer, Arthur Fry, admits that without the option to stay in his field and aspire to become one of 3M's elite "corporate scientists," he would have left lab work and entered management—or quit and started his own business—long before the Post-it idea came to him.

Technical ladders are frequently attempted, then neglected, subject to a once-a-decade revival of interest; most have not lived up to their promise. A Columbia University study found many of them were "parking grounds" for technicians who had failed as managers, rather than fast tracks for the company's most vitally needed technical talent. The problem lies with those who create them more than those who try to scale them. The ladder's effectiveness is frequently diminished by its lack of parity with titles and compensation given to equivalent-level managers. In addition, most technical career paths are criticized for premature topping off. In cultures that share the American value that everyone can become president, this truncated route only creates a caste of second-class citizens.

The problem of stunted advancement results in part from the well-meaning but too narrow motivation behind many of these programs. Often, their explicit purpose is to maintain the morale of scientists and engineers and to avoid their turnover. Implicitly, however, too many have a negative purpose—to keep otherwise ambitious people out of management jobs for which they lack appropriate abilities. This is certainly important, but focusing on the negative purpose tends to limit careful consideration of just how the occupants of places on the second ladder are supposed to be making a contribution. For some, avoiding management responsibilities becomes a way to avoid responsibilities to the company altogether.

Creating dual advancement paths needs to be a business issue, not just a human resources program. It is also an idea with too much potential to remain limited to a company's "techies." A hierarchy of nonmanagement jobs should be available for all professional specialists or knowledge workers.

Empowerment is not a substitute for growth and advancement. Reinforcing jobs allows considerable opportunity for an individual to grow in place by adding breadth and depth to his or her skill base. For many individuals, the advancement opportunities available in the horizontal organization will be sufficient. But some also will have the interest and ability to contribute in the vertical superstructure and in ways other than assuming traditional management accountabilities.

What would such a career structure look like? It would have more of an upright rectangular shape than a pyramidal one. Perhaps it could best be symbolized by a spiral staircase, or double helix—essentially, two long chains twisted around each other. Whatever the shape, as with all structures, organizational or architectural, the way the basic materials are used will determine many of their properties.

Two Ways to Add Value: Bear Loads or Serve as a Veneer

Architects use materials in two ways—for structural purposes or as veneers. When used structurally, a material's main role is to hold the building together, spanning openings or forming columns. When used as a veneer, it need support only its own weight, but it adds value to a building in other important ways. It can modify the building's outward appearance significantly. It can add a sense of texture and depth that might have been impossible to achieve otherwise. As a skin over the load-bearing structure, veneers allow the designer to economically leverage the materials being used. An all-stone or all-brick house is much more costly to build than one with a veneer of these materials over strong but less attractive cinder blocks. As an element of architectural design, the word "veneer' has none of the negative connotation it sometimes acquires in day-to-day usage.

Veneers such as glass can allow light to flow and transform a dark, inward-oriented structure into one better connected with its environment. Veneers also give the builder greater flexibility. Some materials, such as stone, can serve as either veneer or structural elements. When used structurally to make a wall, stone must be of a certain size to support the pieces above and must be arranged in a particular way, with its joints staggered, to maximize its ability to resist cracking. But the same stone, when used as a veneer, allows the architect many more size and placement options; it even can be used primarily for decorative effect, possibly to create a stone mosaic.

There are close parallels between the contrasting roles of structural elements and veneers in a building and the functions of managers and professionals in an organization. Managers must be load-bearing; their deployment determines how a business structures its accountabilities. The nature of their work forces them to focus much of their attention internally. To maximize the strength they provide, their positions have to be structured to minimize organizational brittleness—by limiting the number of managers placed directly above other managers in the structure and by ensuring that each of their levels reflects a discrete time horizon of relevance to the company.

The requirements on independently contributing professionals are different. Their roles can be more flexible. They can focus as much on the world outside the company as on its internal workings. They can act as windows to new markets and capabilities. These are all useful functions, but, like veneers, they cannot stand alone. They need to be plugged firmly into the workings of the rest of the corporation to pay off for the business. Providing those connections is a key job of the management structure. While most corporations have had many years' experience structuring management positions, relatively few have thought out an appropriate business logic for this parallel hierarchy. A good starting point is consideration of the company's future and the role of the professional hierarchy in planning for that future.

Mapping the Business Future on the Professional Track

What about the parallel hierarchy makes it worthwhile from the company's perspective? What is required if the business is to gain from each stage of the hierarchy?

For the dual hierarchy to serve the company, two things need to happen to the work performed by those advancing up the professional track. Like well-structured management work, it must reflect expanding time horizons as the person doing it advances. It also needs to give emphasis to the capabilities that will most strongly drive the business's future.

The considerations about time frame and future orientation are similar to those discussed in Chapter 9. There are a number of benefits that can be attained by having the levels of professional advancement correspond with the time frames associated with each management level. Thus, a company with four levels of management might also have four tiers of advancement possible on its professional track. These might correspond to the time horizons associated with each management level. Most of the professional contributors operating in the one-year or two- to three-year horizons would be in the third phase of their careers (mentors and project managers), whereas those in the five- and ten-year hierarchal levels would be in Phase 4 (directors). Professionals in the earlier career stages would be based in the horizontal organization and most likely associated with a business process manager. Their time frames would vary from one day to several months.

Increases in a professional's time horizon may be manifested in a shift from preoccupation with the needs of today's customers to concern with what those customers will want to buy in the future. The lower levels of the professional hierarchy can include employees with considerable knowledge about current customers and markets, and the senior ones can be more focused on the business's potential markets and new customers. London Business School's Gary Hamel has gone to lengths to bemoan the tendencies of most companies to "work very hard to delineate the executive ownership of existing competitive space. But how many," he asks, "give equal attention to assigning the responsibility for finding and then filling in the white spaces that represent new competitive territory?" This is a role for the company's senior individual contributors, not its senior managers, who are busy focusing on the existing businesses.

Linking Hierarchy With Competitive Capabilities

The framework presented in Chapter 3 for analyzing corporate capabilities can also contribute to helping resolve questions about which professions weigh in at particular levels on the hierarchy and about which viewpoints are most important to reflect where. The issue here is one of what types of knowledge most significantly impact business results over which time frame.

The knowledge professionals who serve as expertise carriers of the capabilities most critical to competitive success should be concentrated at the middle and upper levels of the hierarchy. They need the power that this positioning can provide to ensure their contribution to the company's competitive advantage is leveraged across as much of the business as possible. In contrast, those capabilities that were classified as core and complementary in Chapter 3 are needed to pay off in the short run, so most of the independent contributors associated with them belong on the lower rungs of the professional ladder. Figure 12 illustrates this hierarchy of capabilities, as well as the corresponding management team.

The originators and champions of what have been termed cutting-edge capabilities often appear, surprisingly, at opposite ends of the hierarchy. Some, especially discoverers or inventors, may be at the bottom of the ladder, a great place to nurture new perspectives in employees untainted by years of employment at the company. These fresh views of technology or of the marketplace need to be balanced with some seasoned sponsorship and cross-business long-term perspective, the stock in trade of those at the top of the parallel ladder.

The determination within any company of which capability is core and which critical is always a dynamic one. What is important is that *as a capability's significance to the corporation changes, so do the points at which it needs to be most reflected on the professional hierarchy.* This track cannot

Figure 12. Create a parallel hierarchy.

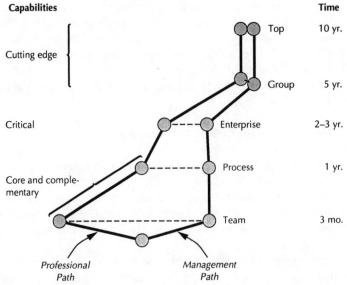

lag too far behind the competitive dynamics of the industry, as happened in the U.S. steel industry in the 1960s, when the upper ends of most corporate hierarchies were wedded to their belief in traditional blast furnace technology and to the view that customers most wanted large and local suppliers of commodity products. Blind spots in their awareness of what was really going on in the industry allowed Asian competitors to export low-priced steel and upstart American companies to pioneer the new minimill technology.

At best, the allocation of professional viewpoints on the parallel hierarchy will happen in advance of changes in the business environment. Since the future is never fully knowable, redundancy is often the best way to avoid being surprised. While establishing extra management posts is costly and is usually accompanied by a blurring of the company's focus, it is relatively easy to add a small number of individually contributing professionals, possibly as side bets on a promising technology or new market, to minimize future lag. These slots can also provide holding zones for some talented deviants, employees who might otherwise become discouraged, eventually leaving to join a competitor or to start a rival business just because there was no place in the corporate structure for them to develop a promising idea.

Alfred Sloan used this approach to great advantage when he ran General Motors. He created an off-the-chart position for Charles Kettering, GM's star inventor at the time, to work on his pet idea of a copper-cooled engine. In doing so, Sloan kept GM's organization focused on gaining market share from Ford by using the established core technology of radiator-cooled motors while allowing Kettering's work to serve as a side bet in case the new approach was ever needed in the marketplace. Apparently, it never was, and Kettering's idea languished. While this move provided some "technology insurance" for GM at the time, such insurance cannot substitute for ideas brought to the development stage. Some critics have attributed GM's 1970s decline in technological innovativeness to its failure to give appropriate power to potential Kettering-like successors.

There's Not Room for Everybody Everywhere

Another critical issue in planning a parallel hierarchy is determining where individual contributors will report. Keep in mind this is an advancement track for nonmanagers, so it will not do for them to be responsible for directing less senior individual contributors. Each individual contributor in this new structure will report to a manager at the next highest time horizon level. Eventually, at Arthur D. Little, Jacques De-cartes's contributions were needed by all the European offices, not just his Belgian home base. So he moved from reporting to the head of the Brussels office to reporting to the managing director for all the company's European operations. (See Chapter 10.)

This discussion of promotion along the professional path is not to be taken to imply that all individual contributors are expected to reach Phase 4 in their careers and to land on the upper rung of their company's ladder. Not all will want to, nor will all be able. And for some who are capable, the areas in which they can best make a contribution will not be of sufficient value to their business to warrant their advancement. The process of resizing, reshaping, and rethinking outlined in this book is a sequential one. The steps must occur in order. Resizing from the top down by pruning capabilities must happen before the hierarchy is laid out. Otherwise, there will be more clutter than even a dual path for advancement can support.

Some professional contributors will pursue interests that leave them knowing more and more about less and less, hardly a situation many companies can afford to reward. Dual ladders allow for greater move-ment and flexibility than more unitary systems, but they do not solve all career advancement problems. They can be just as corrupted by "grade creep" and unwarranted promotion as can management hierarchies. Eternal vigilance, clear and enforced advancement criteria, and the dis-cipline imposed by well-defined differences between each level are man-datory if the integrity of the dual ladder is to be maintained.

The Middle Manager's New Role

Most of the discussion to this point has been about only one side of the advancement track, the path for individual contributors. This is because it is the least developed in most companies. It is also the place from which the greatest future organizational leverage will come. Those on the professional track, burdened with few operational responsibilities, may be very busy trying to change the corporation, rather than control it. But someone still has to be in charge, to be seen as in control.

With all the popular attention provided to worker empowerment and vision-driven leadership from the top, it is not surprising that mid-dle management's role in the new corporation has been ignored. Some management watchers act as though middle management is destined to be replaced by the computer. Tom Peters has called management hier-archies "merely machines that process and agglomerate information, each level adding a further degree of synthesis." Their reason for being recedes, he says, as "we develop technology-based information processing, and especially as we link the systems in networks, inside and outside the corporation."

But, as we pointed out in Chapter 9, hierarchies provide more than information relay and conglomeration. They serve some valuable psychological purposes, and, when well-constructed, *they keep the future from being lost.* As a company builds a horizontal, process-oriented, organization, the role of those managers above it may need to significantly change.

How will it change? Those on the management track will not, through a wave of the magic wand of empowerment, escape responsibility for the results of the organization units they oversee. If anything, they will be held more accountable than ever for them; fewer management layers will make it easier to pinpoint responsibility, allocate praise, and assign blame. It may sound excessively basic to talk about a manager being held accountable to the next level up in the hierarchy for the results of subordinates' work. But more than one senior executive has tried to attribute the company's failings to the performance problems of his subordinates. A chief executive was fired by his board for doing just this; each explanation he provided for missed results stood up individually but, taken together, they indicated the CEO did not know what was personally expected of him. The once popular style of management-by-subordinate commitment has no place in the new corporation.

At Toyota it is very clear who is responsible for the success or failure of every new car introduction. It is the chief engineer assigned to that model. This manager has unusually broad responsibilities that involve almost everything associated with the development of "his" car. He is expected to monitor social, political, and environmental trends. He determines the size and market niche the model is aimed at. He decides which of Toyota's advanced manufacturing practices will be used to make it and which members of its vast supplier network will provide parts. He constantly travels to meet the car dealers and their customers to obtain firsthand feedback on what they like and dislike about existing Toyota models. This information is taken into account when he returns to Toyota City, 300 miles southwest of Tokyo, to approve the marketing strategies his experts have developed to sell the new model.

Jobs with this scope do not exist in Detroit, or in many other car manufacturing capitals. Toyota's structure is an example of middle management potency, a sharp contrast to the too-common pattern of responsibility fragmentation, finger pointing, and crash catch-up programs.

New Middle-Management Tactics

Although a manager's traditional accountabilities will remain unchanged in the future, the tactics used to ensure results will, out of necessity, evolve.

General Electric's chief executive, Jack Welch, is personally spearheading a campaign to convince his managers that their role is no longer to control people and to constantly stay "on top" of all events. Rather, he wants them to focus on guiding, energizing, and exciting those who work in the organizations they manage.

The head of NutraSweet, Robert Shapiro, echoes Welch's concerns and feels he must demand much more from managers than ever before. He says managers have few opportunities in his company to execute clear-cut orders from the top of the hierarchy. Instead, he expects each manager to have a very clear understanding of NutraSweet's strategy and the capabilities needed to achieve it and then to improvise as the immediate situation requires.

This increased emphasis on results, rather than methods, is akin to what some management scholars have described as the best way to manage professionals: Provide them with "envelope supervision." This phrase covers two steps: discussing very carefully with the professionals the minimum information necessary for the manager to feel comfortable that all is on track without eroding discretion within the time horizon in which the professional is expected to contribute, and then establishing with them the limits within which the individual contributor's discretion may be exercised.

Another management practice, advanced many years ago by former AT&T executive Robert Greenleaf, still holds great promise to help the emerging breed of middle managers define their modus operandi. Called by the theologically oriented name "servant leadership," it is an approach based on Greenleaf's observation that often the strongest leadership is provided when the manager is focused on taking care of subordinates and eliciting from them what needs to be done. It fits well with the idea that the horizontal organization is where the real-time action is. One exponent of this philosophy, business school dean Robert Taylor, describes the servant leader as one who has, not the answers, but the right questions. He knows that it is the people in constant contact with customers and technologies who are usually the best source for the answers.

A servant leader allows subordinates to feel "they don't have to go to great lengths making sure they are getting their fair share of resources or rewards, that they don't continually have to waste time watching their backs—because they know their manager is doing these things for them."

This contrasts with the more typical perversion of management hierarchy in which subordinates feel the necessity to spend hours preparing for presentations to top management, because the seniors in the hierarchy act as if they are the consumers of the company's efforts.

Servant leadership might sound wishy-washy on the surface, but it has been practiced with great impact at tough-minded companies like Cypress and Federal Express. Ask a Federal Express employee how many subordinates report to his manager. You will probably hear something like: "Sorry, you seem to have it backwards. My manager works for the twelve of us to help us succeed at our jobs."

Greenleaf's ideas have more depth to them than the popular injunction to behave less like a boss and more like a coach. Still, at least one former practicing coach, Paul "Bear" Bryant of the University of Alabama's football team, has caught the essence of this leadership style in a homily that also summarizes his approach to recognition: "If anything goes bad, I did it. If anything goes semigood, then we did it. If anything goes real good, then you did it."

For a summing up of the role of the new middle manager, see Figure 13.

A flaw in some rosy "middle manager of the future" scenarios is that they carefully specify how the middle manager's role must change, but they then ignore the changes in management structure and hierarchies that also need to occur to provide a firm platform from which the new role is to be played. Both need careful consideration if the new corporation is going to behave as if the future really mattered.

Keeping Both Tracks Roughly Parallel

Dual tracks can go very wrong if their paths diverge. The purpose of parallel hierarchies is to provide for multiple ways, in multiple time

Figure 13. New breed of middle manager.

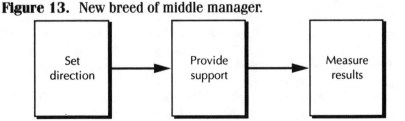

frames, for contributions to be made to an organization's success. The corporate superstructure must have coded within its configuration the knowledge and power necessary to perpetuate the business. Earlier in this chapter, we gave several examples of how this was done at the upper end of the hierarchies at Braun, Microsoft, and TRW. This is a process, though, that has to happen at many points in a company's vertical hierarchy, perhaps analogous to the steps on a spiral staircase that form the cross-links that keep the structure together. Mechanisms such as Arthur D. Little's directorate serve a similar purpose, as does an internal board of directors meant to guide the development of portions of a company's business without adding another senior level of management hierarchy. Germany's Siemens divided its $45 billion corporation into sixteen minicorporations, each with its own leadership team and board of directors. These smaller businesses range from $500 million to $8 billion a year in sales, but the idea can work just as well for much smaller entities.

In the future, it may become common for the originator of a new business idea, if he or she is on the professional track, to organize an internal board, serve as its chair, and "hire" a manager to oversee the idea's development—all with senior management's blessing.

When boards such as these are thoughtfully crafted they should include managers—at the level of, or possibly one level above, the executive being supervised—*and* senior individual contributors. Some may have room for members from outside the corporation, possibly suppliers, customers, or astute market watchers. The board idea is too good to limit to the very top of the company.

At the middle level of the parallel hierarchies, it is important that both sides build and maintain strong relationships by training together. Management development is too useful to provide only to managers; career-phase-specific programs should be devised for all levels in the hierarchy.

Probably the best way to prevent the development of two diverging cultures is to move people back and forth regularly from one hierarchy to the other. At Arthur D. Little, Jacques Decartes's longtime hierarchal superior, the head of the Brussels office, eventually moved to an individual contributor position concerned with building one of the company's newest and most promising practice areas. He was replaced, not by Decartes, who was firmly tied to his role as a senior professional, but by another Belgian who formerly had had responsibility for strategic planning for the company throughout Europe.

IBM and Xerox regularly use similar cross-hierarchy moves. An IBM technical contributor may rotate, with the prior assistance of a well-planned management skill acquisition program, to a managerial slot, with the eventual goal of returning to the professional track with an increased awareness of the management role, an awareness that can come only from rolling up one's sleeves and joining in the work.

These kinds of spiraling career progressions will become increasingly important as unneeded management levels disappear and as advancement from one level of management to another becomes more of a broad jump than a continuously progressing hop. These wide gaps, measured in broadened time horizons of responsibility, may require an advancement-oriented manager to move first to a professional contributor position at his or her current level, where the manager can serve as an assisting understudy to a manager one level up. A series of successful same-level management slot rotations also may be required before a candidate is considered for hierarchal movement.

Many other creative and mutually beneficial career movements are possible when a parallel hierarchy is a key component of organizational infrastructure. Other elements of the corporate infrastructure can also benefit from the kind of rethinking that has been applied here to provide two paths to the top. Just as the integrity and strength of a structure derives from the materials used to make it, the functionality of a structure is often determined by how well the design of its infrastructure was thought out.

Chapter 12
Question All the Answers

Replace jobs with assignments and monopolies with free markets; never let managers stay in one job too long; and be sure to test the new organization before implementing.

Amsterdam's ING Bank building was mentioned in Chapter 1 as a physical embodiment of the idea of an "architecture of change." This headquarters building has been well *sized*. It provides work space for more than 2,000 employees in a structure that does not overwhelm the residential and shopping district in which it is located. Its *shape*, like Fallingwater's, is predominantly horizontal, allowing for easy movement from office to office and department to department. As with some of the most innovative houses of Frank Lloyd Wright, the Dutch architect of the ING Bank minimized the occurrence of right angles throughout the structure, another way to speed movement and encourage pedestrian circulation both within the building and outside it.

The ING building also symbolizes well the *rethinking* process. Its infrastructure is as innovative as is its superstructure. An interior walkway, with floors of Italian stone and walls lined with art and plants, links the ten minitowers of the building. More than just an office building corridor, clusters of comfortable chairs and tables are included throughout to encourage impromptu networking. For more lengthy informal conferences, a snack bar, four restaurants, and several gardens tucked into the building's external folds are available.

This is a building that seems to question all the traditional answers about building design. In addition to multifunctional passageways, the role of stairways, wall color, and even wall shape have been rethought. Staircases are wide, covered with glass domes to fill them with daylight, and are placed in ways that encourage their regular use, not just their serving as a hidden backup for use when the elevators break down. Careful thought has been given to the color of the interior walls. Those on the cold north side of the building are painted in warm earth tones. The structure's sunnier south side features cooler grays and blues. Few of the building's external walls are vertical. This makes it appear less massive and also reduces neighborhood noise pollution by reflecting sound upward. And, since the walls are angled to the sun, they help the building absorb additional rays, reducing heating costs.

Perhaps the kind of rethinking process that guided the design of ING Bank's headquarters can also be applied in the realm of organizational architecture. The experience a company gains in rethinking career structures and the role of hierarchy can launch a reexamination of other management practices that have been taken for granted for too long. Opportunities for doing this abound.

Areas Ripe for Rethinking

Every business has its dysfunctions. Some have always been sources of difficulty; others have become such with the adoption of new, leaner ways of organizing. Some are so fundamental to how companies have successfully operated in the past that they are worthy of special attention. What follows are examples of several such areas that are ripe for rethinking. Most companies will find this list easily expandable.

First, let's reexamine the idea that a company is a collection of individual jobs or positions. This proposition is usually accepted without any second thought. It is also a lot of nonsense.

Replace Jobs With Assignments

Businesses that have focused their capabilities, organized around processes, and tamed their hierarchy are ready for a more far-reaching change—the elimination of all jobs.

Lest the wrong idea be conveyed, please note the target here is jobs and positions, not employees and employment. Employees who are loyal to the business because the business is loyal to them are absolutely vital. Providing employment, compensation keyed to contribution, and some assurance that both will continue or help will be provided if one or both are eliminated are key elements of the mutual loyalty pact. In exchange, however, many employers may find it necessary to rethink how work gets done and to look for ways beyond traditionally structured positions to both maximize flexibility and ensure the company is making use of the full range of employees' skills.

In most companies, work is packaged into eight-hour-a-day, forty-hour-a-week positions. Occasionally these positions are divided in half, or by some fraction close to it, providing a minimal measure of flexibility to employer and employee. At times, position descriptions and management-by-objectives are used as guides, although too often, after some brief orientation, the nature of "the job" is taken for granted. So is its permanency. Increasingly frequent reorganizations notwithstanding, most companies act as if a position is to last forever. This message is conveyed to employees, and it shapes their own expectations about work and careers. The best way to change your job is by promotion, the conventional wisdom says, even though possibilities for advancement are becoming increasingly limited in many organizations. Reorganization provides some employees with advancement opportunities, albeit usually at a cost of considerable anxiety and disruption.

Change is hard, partly because positions do tend to take on a life of their own, sometimes independent of their intended contribution to the business. They become animate objects, possessions that are "owned" by their incumbents and bargained or fought over. (This is one reason why head count change becomes the most measured objective of many restructurings.) Their implied permanence leads them to be defined more by their boundaries than their results, creating another wall between employees and what needs to get done.

What alternatives are available? Chapter 6 described one—surrendering one's individual job for membership in a "composite team." It is, when fully developed, a very useful idea—but not for everyone, or for every type of work. It is a form of job sharing, appropriate when the work to be done is "bigger" than any one individual can handle. A lot of work, though, comes most naturally in chunks smaller than the capacity of an employee. Let's call these chunks *assignments*.

Whereas a job is a laundry list of activities, an assignment is more focused. It has a clear result. The result can be measured, so it is apparent when the assignment is over. A job—barring a serious downsizing or an act of God—goes on forever. Some are even inherited. An assignment is always time-bounded. It has a beginning, a middle, and an end; it follows a life cycle. Assignments are like many consumer products. They have shelf lives (or half lives), beyond which they start to go stale.

A company that wanted to eliminate all jobs could move the employees into teams, possibly along the lines of the innovative Japanese ceramics maker Kyocera. This Kyoto-headquartered high-tech company sorts everyone into groups comprising from two or three employees to several hundred. Each group has a clear objective, allowing its contribution to Kyocera's profitability to be measured (and the company's accounting system has been structured around the necessity to do this).

These teams are formed and dissolved as business needs require; none is expected to be permanent. See Figure 14 for an illustration of the alternatives I have just discussed to traditional job structure.

In surveys in which Japanese executives were asked to name the company they admired most for entrepreneurship and technology leadership, Kyocera ranked ahead of better-known companies such as Honda or Sony. This reputation is due in part to these unconventional management practices, ones that make it a maverick among Japanese companies.

On the other side of the Pacific, a Silicon Valley maverick, Cypress Semiconductors, has pioneered a system of self-imposed goal setting for all employees that is updated weekly. Coordinated through simple personal computer-based software, every Monday all employees provide a priority-ranked list of what they will accomplish over the next month and a half, as well as updates on the status of previous goals. These are computer-consolidated that night and available to all managers the next day so they can sort out conflicts, identify slippages, and see what assistance they need to provide to those who work for them. Every Wednesday Cypress's chief executive has a companywide status report on these assignments. This provides him with an "organizational speedometer" and gives an early warning of cross-department slippages that may affect businesswide performance. Most important, this system also allows the company to be project- rather than job-driven, an essential in an industry that puts a premium on speed and flexibility.

Problems can emerge with systems like this if top management attempts to micromanage the work of its subordinates or misses changes in the forest because of a preoccupation with the trees. Still, these systems can provide a useful control infrastructure for an assignment-driven business.

Figure 14. Alternatives to traditional job structure.

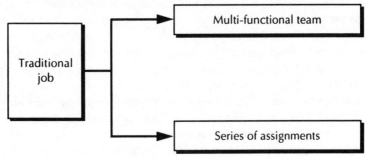

This is not only a high-technology computer parts maker's practice. Look over the shoulder of what appears to be one of the night-shift guards at Chaparral Steel. You may well find the person, in addition to watching the automated security monitors, entering the previous day's orders and quality results into the plant computer system. The guard may take an exercise break to fill the fire extinguishers, and he is also trained to perform checks on the machinery that is idled for the night. Is this one job, or is it a start at creating a series of assignments for what would otherwise be a sleepy, dead-end position?

In companies built around assignments, *each employee has a portfolio of projects, not a job description.* The size and content of the portfolio varies considerably among employees, depending on factors such as past performance on similar tasks, assessments of potential, education and related experience, personal interest, and availability. Managers need to look more closely at the characteristics of the work and the way they package it. Some companies give considerable attention to assessing and categorizing their employees, with tools such as Myers-Briggs indicators and managerial grids. Getting all a company's work done through assignments requires careful analysis of the characteristics of the work as well as of the workers.

Managers and employees operating in this environment need to become master schedule jugglers. Each employee's portfolio is dynamic, not static. At any one point in time an individual's portfolio may have an assignment just starting, one or two half-completed, and another winding down. The trick in scheduling is to avoid having all of any one person's tasks in the same stage of completion—something much easier to hope for than achieve.

Applying this philosophy works best on an all-or-nothing basis. Its full value as an organizing tool cannot be realized if it is just a special projects overlay on traditional position description-driven jobs. This means adopting a new mind-set about ongoing, taken for granted tasks: *They do not exist anymore.* Companies that have adopted the continuous improvement doctrine in their quality programs should find this easy. Every task is associated with a time frame. In addition to completing the task, or several iterations of it, during the time period, the employee is also expected to have made some measurable improvement in the quality or productivity associated with the task.

The important thing here is the specification of a time boundary for everything. *It gets done, gets better, or both.* This can have an amazing impact on focusing attention and improving performance—if it is real and well-managed. Similar to the crystallizing effect of an appointment with the hangman, thoughtful deadlines can be powerful tools for converting mundane routine into meaningful accomplishment.

Both General Motors and Northern Telecom have been surprised by this phenomenon when they conducted "nontraditional" plant closings—nontraditional in that they gave many more months' notice that the plants would be shut down than is commonly provided or legally required. Both companies found that during the period from when the notice was provided to the actual closing, the plants' *productivity soared!* Absenteeism and scrap rate dropped, and product quality and morale were frequently the best ever.

Why these counterintuitive results? For the first time in these plants' histories, *time* was really being managed the way it should be. Knowing when "the assignment" had to end provided a strong focus for everybody's attention and efforts. Knowing the length of the game seemed to motivate the players to give it their best. This aspect of worker psychology is so useful that it is well worth applying to other situations. Replacing jobs with time-bounded assignments can be a good way to do so.

Thinking about a person's employment along these lines can offer a number of benefits to the employee. Once the forty-hour workweek mold is broken, it is much easier to provide employment in smaller chunks of time. For many employees, especially those with young children and members of two-wage-earner families, part-time work has great potential attractiveness—as long as it does not imply accepting a sentence to career Siberia. Managing employees through assignment completion rather than job occupancy redefines what constitutes acceptable performance, reducing the need to distinguish between full- and part-time employees. For the same reason, it also can facilitate telecommuting and greater flexibility in work hours, both popular alternatives for many employees.

This conversion provides a number of advantages to employers willing to make the required upgrade of their management practices. Cost savings are certainly possible through increased use of part-time employees, even when they receive the pro-rated benefits vital to keep from creating a second class of employees. Increased flexibility in coping with workload changes and differing skill requirements also offers the possibility of achieving the same work with lower payroll costs. Organizing this way is good preparation for choosing tasks to assign to temporary or contingent workers (sometimes the best of whom are recycled retirees).

This approach is a change that supports (and also depends on) contemporary innovations in compensation, such as those that move toward providing fewer but broader "bands" of pay levels and establishing base salaries that are determined more by skills and know-how than by job title.

Institute Term Appointments for Every Manager

The ideas we've been discussing apply to management work just as much as they do to work done by an individual contributor. Organizing a company along these lines implies that each manager has a clearly defined time period in which he or she is expected to hold a particular position, related, if possible, to the time horizon applicable to the level in the hierarchy being occupied (see Chapter 9 for more information about time horizons). Associated with this period are one or two priority missions that the manager is expected to achieve: turning around a troubled operation, making a significant improvement in cost and product quality, successfully introducing a new product, or capturing a specified fraction of the market by a certain time, for example. These missions are not all that is expected of the manager. However, if missions are established for every position, they can set a theme that gives shape and focus to the person's tenure—something missing in many management jobs today.

When the mission is completed, it is hoped close to schedule, it is time to move on—perhaps to another management job at the same level in need of that individual's special talents, perhaps to a senior individual contributor's slot, or possibly to an understudy post in preparation for advancement up the management hierarchy. One of the greatest errors companies make is *keeping managers in place long after the reason they were selected becomes irrelevant*. Not having a preset, multiyear "term appointment" sends the implicit message the job is available for life—or at least until some dreadful mistake is made. This is not the disciplined, performance-driven orientation most companies want to cultivate. Yet it is almost inevitable unless at the outset of a manager's appointment some sense of duration is provided as the context in which the manager's multiyear mission is laid out and committed to. Of course, in some situations the manager may move on sooner or she may be asked to stay for another round, but at least an explicit framework is available in which to make such decisions.

The rapid growth of the temporary, or interim, management industry is an indication of the increasing acceptance of assignments as replacements for jobs as ways to get things done. It is now possible to "rent" a chief financial officer or a seasoned division head who already has accomplished an important mission similar to the one facing the renting company. The industry is built on the kind of rethinking that says: "We need a market plan, not necessarily a market planner; a turn-around, not a turnaround artist; or a brochure, not a brochure writer." Reorganizing around time-bounded assignments can pave the way for an important, related area of rethinking: questioning the necessity for doing everything in-house.

Replace Monopolies With Free Markets

Interim management is just a special case of a much larger phenomenon: outsourcing. Like all popular trends, outsourcing, or contracting out, has its pluses and minuses. It is not a one-size-fits-all solution for orga-nization bloat. There are too many contradictory rules for when it is appropriate; every candidate for outsourcing needs to be considered on its individual merits.

Outsourcing can be useful when the need is temporary or cyclical—or when the need is ongoing but is not one of the five or six key business processes most worth organizing around. It is indicated when work is not highly critical to competitive success—and also when it is so critical that the only way to get something done is to go outside the company. The computer this book was written on, a Macintosh Powerbook 100, is part of the Apple family of notebooks. But its design and manufacture were subcontracted to Sony, a strategy used by Apple to speed its entry into a critical market segment.

Outsourcing can make sense when a skill is so common that it di-verts attention from other, more vital skills on whose development the business needs to focus. Conversely, a skill may be so rare or impossible to retain internally that outsourcing is the only way to obtain it.

Despite these complexities, the kind of company that can be created through intelligent and selective outsourcing is one well worth having. It is one that has eliminated its internal monopolies.

It is ironic that so many otherwise free enterprise-oriented execu-tives tolerate vast, closed marketplaces within their companies. These are their internal service-providing units. They all have customers; the customers just happen to be employees of the business. Unfortunately, because of the monopolistic quality, many companies have to put up with second-class service—and tolerate higher-than-necessary over-head. In the United States, improvement in white-collar productivity is almost nil, one reason overhead takes a bigger bite out of American manufacturers' revenues than it does from their European or Japanese competitors.

Internal monopolies are expensive luxuries. The watchdog arm of the U.S. government, the General Accounting Office, examined the operations of the federal in-house printing operation, the Government Printing Office (GPO). Its verdict: "The GPO, established as a near-monopoly in 1861 to provide efficient government printing services, has become a huge, inefficient enterprise that last year billed its customers double what they would have paid commercial printers." The GPO was found over time to have perpetuated inefficiency because of its insulation from market forces.

This is not just a government problem. It is difficult to find a corporation without its own array of GPO-like functions. The real trick, though, is to keep the cure from being worse than the disease. The too-common remedy has been near-mindless overhead reductions—programs that seldom face up to the real issue of just what businesses (serving internal as well as external customers) the company should be in.

A better idea is to eliminate organizational backwaters, *to make your low-priority activity someone else's high priority.* This is the essence of what contractors like ServiceMaster try to provide. For some of their customers, they serve as a managerial intermediary, providing supervision, labor-saving tools, and training for a hospital's janitorial work force. While it may be pointless for a hospital to make capital or knowledge investments in janitorial jobs, for companies like ServiceMaster it is the source of their future competitiveness.

Sometimes a company like Xerox takes over responsibility for the internal service functions of another company, as it has done at Bankers Trust. There Xerox operates a diverse but information-related group of activities (mailroom, printshop, payroll, employee record keeping, central phone switchboard), employing the ex-Bankers Trust employees who formerly provided these services. The pattern is increasingly common: Bankers Trust, in turn, manages, on a contract basis, the employee savings and retirement programs of many Fortune 500 companies, work once done by these company's employees.

It is as if many companies are "getting in each other's pockets" in order to allow each company to focus its own employees primarily in ways that add the greatest value to its outside customers. Pitney Bowes employees deliver the mail at IBM offices, while IBM employees staff the Kodak data processing center. Recently the glass manufacturer Libby-Owens-Ford literally sold its information systems department and its mainframe computer to the former head of this function at the company. He formed an outsourcing company to sell data processing services back to his former employer, as well as to other companies. His outsourcing company is in the business of writing computer programs and providing reports that its clients need, not running computers. So it, in turn, got rid of the mainframe it purchased and is outsourcing the computer operations portion of its business to a more focused provider of that particular service.

In contrast to the *make it someone else's problem* approach, some companies are following a *take in each other's laundry* strategy. Global electrical equipment maker ABB reduced what was a 6,000-employee headquarters function to require fewer than 200 positions. This was accomplished, in part, by creating service-oriented businesses to do what was once handled by overhead-funded staff. ABB Marketing Services is one of these new businesses. It is run like an enterprise unit. It creates and manages advertising campaigns for ABB's other businesses, it also works for outside clients—and it is also expected to make money. Italian tire maker Pirelli followed the same path when it told its strategic planners they were no longer to sit at headquarters and pass judgment on the plans submitted by Pirelli's divisions. Instead, they were to sell their planning services, on the same fee basis as is used by outside consultants, to the divisions. The divisions were free to use the outsiders, if they preferred, or to do all the work themselves. To help establish its bona fides as recognized experts to the divisions, the former headquarters planning group also sells its services to businesses outside the Pirelli group.

Probably the world's two largest debureaucraticization efforts are proceeding on similar lines. As massive government-owned conglomerates in what was East Germany are dismantled, many workers are encouraged to form independent service and technical support companies. About 2,000 of the optics company Carl Zeiss Jena's 60,000 employees accepted such encouragement, which comes with low-cost loans and equipment and facility leases to help ease the transition. IBM's massive restructuring includes setting up subsidiaries around the world to sell, on an arm's-length basis, services that were once provided internally. Its new Workforce Solutions unit includes 1,400 former IBM human resources specialists who provide pay and benefits administration and management training to the IBM units in which they were formerly based.

Monopoly busting is not limited to situations involving thousands of workers. It is often a good idea to apply one employee at a time. Toro, a Minnesota maker of lawn mowers, fosters innovation by supplementing its inside product development teams with an independent inventor kept on retainer. Bob Comer, who has been on contract for twenty-three years, prefers to work this way. It keeps him focused on his task, not on the office's politics. It also puts a safe distance between him and disapproving executives who might kill a fledgling idea before it is fully developed.

As with all good ideas, internal privatization has its limits. It is no quick fix, and it is dangerous to approach it as such. Its success requires continual oversight and an industry of service providers, not just the exchange of one form of monopoly for another. Most important, it requires careful choices about what is appropriate to do outside the business and what needs to be done internally. Using the topology presented in Chapter 3, many complementary capabilities are good possibilities for outsourcing, whereas critical capabilities almost never are. Core and cutting-edge competences need to be considered individually. Typically, when Japanese companies are on the receiving end of an outsourcing arrangement they see it as a learning opportunity, not as someone else's drudge work. Your company may usefully follow the strategy of outsourcing an activity to a superior provider for a period of time, learning from them how to upgrade your approach, and then decide to bring some or all of the work back inside. Harvard Business School's Michael Porter's research warns that innovating to offset local disadvantages almost always pays off better than outsourcing.

Approaching this issue creatively requires first determining where overhead and support activities occur within your business. If you like to think of them as fat, as many do, remember that despite its harmful effects when eaten in large quantities, some amount of fat intake is useful for good health. And that fat does not just occur around the edges of a piece of meat, as reengineering advocates are quick to point out; it is often interspersed throughout. Locating all this marbling is the first step.

Then keep in mind that free markets work only when they include more than one strong player. Looking outside the company is one way to locate the players; so is "insourcing"—converting units formerly on the overhead dole to quasi-free market operators.

Dramatic changes may be possible; look at what happened when the city of Phoenix started a bidding process to contract out the garbage collection services that the city had always provided. Initially, private waste haulers won contracts for many of the routes put out to bid. But the enterprising director of the Public Works Department did not roll over and play dead. He carefully observed the management practices used by the private operators and went them one better by sending study teams to other cities with especially efficient operations. As the private contracts came up for renewal, armed with these insights, he prepared plans that allowed his municipal operation to outbid the competition. Over ten years, his operation won back every contract it had lost and was the only service-providing part of the Phoenix government to have lowered its unit costs each year.

Try Before You Buy

A building is an expensive thing to get wrong. Just ask the embarrassed owner of the architectural award-winning John Hancock Tower in Boston when its glass-paneled walls started falling to the streets below. Or consider the concerns of the citizens of thirteenth-century Pisa, Italy, when the bell tower being constructed in the town's main square started tilting (at least until the possibilities for increased tourist traffic became more apparent).

Minimizing mishaps like these is a prime concern of architects. Before a building's plans are finalized, careful testing will have been done of the soil conditions, seasonal weather variations will have been taken into account, and possibly building models will have been constructed to allow for wind-tunnel testing. These efforts will be doubled if new building materials are to be used or if the terrain is especially difficult.

These early models, and their accompanying sketches, have another purpose. They are selling tools; they are usually necessary to convince the owner-to-be to hire the architect or to construct the building a certain way. Often competitions are held to choose from among several architects' plans. Some high-visibility projects may even impanel a jury of leading citizens or of future users of the building to select among the prototypes advanced.

Unfortunately, seldom is equivalent care given to testing and evaluating new approaches to corporate organization before they are installed. At times, great efforts are made to solicit ideas for improvements from the occupants of the current organization, but then the redesign process is clouded in secrecy while the planners and the decision makers hurriedly huddle to balance political practicalities with strategic needs. Then the new structure is unveiled, criticism usually muted lest it be taken as a sign of disloyalty, and a resigned spirit of "let's at least give it our best shot" guides the implementation.

Imagine what buildings would look like if their design proceeded along those lines. Perhaps this process explains why so many reorganizations fail to meet expectations or why restructuring seems to be a near-annual event in many companies. What makes this situation especially troubling is that, in other aspects of corporate operations, a great deal of skill and experience is applied to introducing change.

Consider what happens when a new product is launched. Many mock-ups and prototypes are built and rigorously tested. If the product has a connection to an outside regulatory group, its certification will be sought. It is the subject of extensive market research (while still in the idea stage), focus group input, and eventually trial exposure in hand-picked test markets. Then what is learned is carefully evaluated and necessary readjustments made before the product is rolled out to the marketplace. Extensive advertising and other communication efforts accompany the launch, and special promotions are developed to help win customer acceptance. Multiyear market share targets are set, and a schedule is set for periodic product improvement and redesign.

Ironically, even in companies that have mastered processes as complex as these, there are few counterparts to any of these steps when a reorganization is launched (see Figure 15). What is especially missing is any well-managed prototype development and testing. Too often, only limited benchmarking is substituted ("This organization structure seemed to work wonders for IBM. Let's give it a shot").

Often, the closest thing to a prototype produced before a reorganization is a draft organization chart. These charts, while common

Figure 15. Examples of the rethinking process.

Replace:	With:
Tall hierarchies with overlapping responsibilities	Flatter hierarchies with discrete time horizons per level
Managers as the only employees with "real power"	A dual hierarchy of professionals and managers
Jobs	Assignments
Indefinite-term management appointments	Prespecified durations for each management assignment
Overhead monopolies	Free markets for internally needed services
Flying blind into a major reorganization	Trial runs for new organization concepts

enough, are poor representations of most organization structures. They attempt to show in two dimensions (subdivisions and hierarchy) something that must function well in at least three (subdivisions, hierarchy, and *work flows*) and usually four (these three plus *time*).

The problem is similar to that faced by architects. They seldom have trouble visualizing three-dimensional buildings and how the structures will function just by looking at floor plans and side views. But their clients frequently do. Many creative ideas never leave the blueprint stage because they cannot be adequately communicated to the people paying for their implementation.

These difficulties are compounded in the corporate world, where the difficult-enough-to-understand organization chart is invariably marked "Top Secret" and its distribution kept limited, possibly because it is such a poor communication tool that its only significance is as a political document.

Getting around these limitations requires some of the tools of the architect or the new-product developer. Models must be built, reactions sought far and wide, and then the prototypes debugged. Here, the architects have it easier than some corporate planners. They can usually accomplish all this with cleverly drawn sketches and small, three-dimensional models made of paper and wood.

What would be the equivalent of the architect's scale model? Since the organization is essentially a container of human behavior and interactions, perhaps the careful creation of a drama depicting the functioning of the new corporation would best fit the bill. Ideally, it should be written in at least three acts to bring in the time dimension. Several carefully monitored performances should be provided to audiences around the company, and possibly to a few trusted outside critics. After all, shows are not real life; they elicit only temporary involvement and are relatively easy to critique.

While this idea has possibilities, keep in mind we already require the organization planner to be part psychologist, part business planner, part social worker (and now, part architect). Asking also for the skills of a playwright might be excessive. A middle ground is available, though. Most corporations maintain a group of management training or development experts. At times they are brought in after a reorganization is announced to help guide its implementation. Good idea, but bad timing. The best of these specialists are well acquainted with techniques such as computer simulations, multiple-day management "games," and the case method of teaching. At the minimum, a business school-style case could be written of the reorganization under consideration, describing it as if it already were in place. The case could be "taught" widely around the company, with "student" solutions to it factored into creation of the next prototype.

After several rounds of this have occurred, an investment may be justified in a "game" that simulates, with a speeded-up clock, the decisions to be made and the relationships that must work right for the new organization to be successful. Played with many cross-sectional groupings of employees from all levels and segments of the business, it can also prove to be an invaluable debugging device, as well as a way to use the force of anticipation to pave the path for eventual rapid implementation.

The hottest preview tool becoming available for the architect is something called *virtual reality*. A form of computer-assisted simulation, it allows the viewer to grasp reality through microchip-generated illusion. It will eventually allow a prospective building owner to feel as if he or she is walking through the building, complete with all attendant sights, sounds, and feelings ordinarily obtained from touching the proposed wall surfaces or floor coverings. All these variables can be manipulated by changes in the computer software, allowing for many prototype buildings to be "experienced" without a shovel ever coming near the building site.

This is the ultimate "try before you buy." It is another idea too good for organization planners to allow architects to keep to themselves. The new kinds of organization that can be invented with interactive simulation tools such as these will easily outimplement and outperform any management guru's latest solo vision. The shaping process is ultimately more important than any particular shape it produces.

Epilogue

Build Domes, Not Pyramids

Choose a shape for the corporate superstructure that is both strong and economical.

Eventually, the new, creative organization forms that emerge from the prototyping and testing processes described in Chapter 12 will need a sense of direction if they are to pay off economically. For a clue about the structural form most able to gets its arms around all the energy and diversity abundant in a company that has resized, reshaped, and re-thought itself, consider the experience of Microsoft.

This is a company that models its hierarchy after that of a law firm and its horizontal organization, on the amoeba. Its founder, Bill Gates, found it necessary, despite what is arguably the world's most effective E-mail system, to ensure that Microsoft had a once-a-year event bringing all 7,000 employees together under one roof. This allowed, at least potentially, everyone to see everyone else face-to-face.

What structure did Gates use to accommodate this?

A *dome*, of course—in this case, Seattle's large sports stadium, the Kingdome.

The Dome—A Structure for Our Time

Gates might have stumbled onto something when he chose a domed structure for his companywide meeting. Domes have a long history of serving as efficient and beautiful enclosures of space. Just visualize the Pantheon or St. Peter's in Rome or Florence's dramatic symbol of the Renaissance, the Cathedral of Santa Maria del Fiore. Consider the U.S. Capitol's rotunda or that other great icon of American culture, the Houston Astrodome. Their common shape is symbolically uplifting as well as functionally practical. *These characteristics are as important to organization structures as they are to architectural ones.* Domes are structural configurations worthy of close examination to understand how they work.

Domes are half-spheres, or a close variation of this shape. They are very efficient configurations because they are *extremely thin compared to the distances they span.* If an arch-shaped structure, or pyramid, were to cover the same space as a dome, it would have to be ten times as thick to support itself. Perhaps it would even need a supplemental external skeleton, like the Gothic cathedral's flying buttress, to do the job.

What is it about the structure of a dome that makes it so strong? Look up at a domed roof from inside the building. You will most likely see a series of raised ribs radiating from its center downward along the dome's inside. These vertical sections are like the meridians on a globe. You will also likely see a series of parallel hooplike ribs starting at the bottom of the dome and continuing upward. They, in circles of decreasing radii, are the latitudinal lines of the dome. (See Figure 16).

Together, these meridians and parallels (which in some buildings are covered for decorative purposes) form a strong inner grid, a semicircular cobweb. The meridians distribute the dome's weight downward. The horizontal hoops keep this pressure from putting a bulge in the dome's top or from spreading apart its bottom. The net result is a very stable structure, one of the stiffest and strongest ever devised.

As with all structures, the materials used to construct the dome are very important. Many Roman and Renaissance domes eventually developed cracks at their base. Their stone and concrete could not resist the

Figure 16. The infrastructure of a dome.

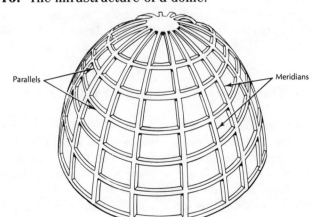

tensions they endured as they resisted the dome's natural tendency to expand at its base. This problem was finally remedied in the nineteenth century when steel rings were used to circle the bottom of the dome, just as steel hoops hold together a wooden barrel.

These tensions and pressures acting on architectural domes are not unlike those affecting many corporate structures. If strong lateral linkages are not present at several levels of a corporate structure to disperse pressures, those pressures are likely to be felt on both the top and the bottom of the company. At the top, a bulge often occurs when these horizontal coordinating mechanisms are weak or nonexistent. Senior executives are overworked and find their attention is frequently distracted when they attempt to solve problems or mesh operations that should have been dealt with at lower levels. To cope with all this, they may hire more headquarters staff or put expensive electronic information systems in place, both of which only tend to expand the bulge.

At the bottom, the lack of discipline and focus that should be provided by the mid-level horizontal linkages can cause an organization to extend its boundaries excessively. Companies without good mechanisms to maintain focus often become victims of unrelated diversification and a tendency to provide all support services internally. The brittleness caused by narrow jobs and fragmented management responsibilities exacerbates these problems.

Domes are not completely flat structures, though. Their purpose is to contain and focus, not to smother. Putting a domelike superstructure over a horizontally oriented group of enterprise units, internal service providers, work processes, expanded jobs, and teams is a useful way to channel their efforts over the long haul. The cross-connected lattice created by the interplay of managerial and professional hierarchies can add a great deal of strength to an organization.

Variations at the Top of the Dome

A dome's upper surface allows for a variety of options. Some, like the U.S. Capitol, have a statue perched atop the building. Many have just a ring of bricks or stones. A few, like the Pantheon, feature a circular opening, an eye to let the strong sun that shines over Rome enter the building.

This kind of versatility can be important for the top of a corporate structure, as well. Many companies are headed by a single, very powerful chief executive. This is the traditional American model, typified by the Lee Iacoccas, Harold Geneens, and Jack Welches. At times top leaders are able to form a creative partnership with an effective No. 2 person. Examples of this useful, but unfortunately rare, complementarity include Coca-Cola's team of Roberto Goizueta and Donald Keough and the Michael Eisner-Frank Wells combination at the Walt Disney Company. But still, totem poles are rarely found atop a dome's peak.

Some companies are finding more utility in a European model of governance: the managing board acting as a team that provides consensus-driven leadership. This is the mode of a Siemens or a Royal Dutch Shell. They have their leaders, but they tend to be called speakers, not chief executives. They are the shapers of the top's consensus, able to work well in a realm of collective responsibility. The domes over these companies are capped with a ring.

A few other companies seem to have strong positions in their industries and an array of customer-pleasing products and services, but an almost invisible top management. They, like Delta Airlines, seem to have mastered the trick of keeping the top leader in the background and putting the spotlight on the employees. Unlike others in what seems to be a heavily ego-driven industry, Delta's chief executives are almost unknown to the flying public, though the airline is the largest flying across the Atlantic and a longtime customer service award winner.

The economy and strength of the dome makes it a much better metaphor for the shape of the new corporation than that provided by the traditional pyramid. Think about the sense of freedom, and even wonder, that can be felt when entering the Pantheon or other world-renowned domed structures. Contrast this with the sense of confinement—or oppression—experienced within a pyramid as its walls seem to close in. This feeling recalls their original purpose: providing a gravesite for Egypt's kings. Companies that operate in the increasing number of unforgiving, globalizing marketplaces may find that clinging too long to a dysfunctional pyramid leaves them with an organization whose only use is to serve as a memorial to their past.

Architecture as a Metaphor

This has been a book about the organizational architecture of the new corporation. Throughout, references have been made to the process and the concerns of building architects as they design physical structures to contain human activities. They select a site, prepare it, plan a structure, and incorporate an infrastructure. They are concerned with the architecture of change, as well as with the architecture of stability.

There are many parallels between this process and the sequence followed by thoughtful executives concerned with getting their organization right: Resize—strategically and operationally; then reshape; and, finally, rethink. The architectural metaphor has been used to stimulate new thinking about what has too often become a unidimensional, one-shot mechanistic process. By thinking differently about what needs to go on when reorganizing, top management may find that it skips fewer critical steps and retains more of the creativity of the designer.

Some buildings look as though they just happened, whereas others seem more "architectural." What is the difference? Architecture is not, as the Canadian architect Witold Rybczynski likes to stress, something just added to plain buildings to make them appear interesting. It is more like the difference between gastronomy and cooking. Both meet basic needs, but one fuses science and artistry in a carefully preplanned manner; the other seems to just happen as necessity dictates. Both buildings and organizations are settings for human activity. But poorly designed ones put obstacles in the way of activity, whereas thoughtfully planned ones can help it flow almost effortlessly.

Even good architecture cannot resist time. Look at the Parthenon, erected in the age of Pericles at Athens's cultural apogee and now a shell providing hints of its former beauty—a victim of several civil wars and centuries of tourists. Frank Lloyd Wright's roofs are reputed to leak occasionally. Even the Pompidou Center in Paris, a modern-art museum built in 1977 that appears to hang all its infrastructure on the outside walls, sometimes looks a little worse for the wear. Buildings require continual maintenance and renovation. So does organizational architecture. If nothing else, functions, strategies, and markets may change long before a hierarchy collapses.

Keeping an organization updated and fully functional requires the same effort that goes into painting a long bridge. By the time a crew has gone from one end to the other, it is usually time to start over on the original side. USAA, the San Antonio insurance company, uses the same principle to keep its organization improvement unit perpetually busy. A year or two after working with one of its internal clients, the group is back to evaluate what has worked and what has not and to help invent remedies for unwanted second-order effects of otherwise good recommendations. Not only must this be an ongoing practice, but it needs to be done with full awareness that the organizational problems being experienced today most likely had their seeds planted years ago when they were the solutions to the pressing problems of that time.

Architecture is big-picture work. Seasoned designers and rebuilders know how difficult it is to change just one thing. Moving just one wall may involve a dozen other structural and infrastructural changes. A key skill of the architect is to think through all these interconnections *before* the first change is made. Capable organizational architects have the same requirement. They do not attempt to restructure jobs before unnecessary work is outplaced; they know that until reinforced jobs and load-bearing managers are in place, it is fruitless to eliminate functional departments and build the organization around business processes.

Lower Walls, Build Bridges

Organization—its structure and the processes it accommodates—is important in itself. It is not just a tool to serve other ends. While it is a key means of generating economic wealth, it is also a place where many people live out much of their lives. This other dimension implies that organization planners have a special responsibility to create something that is not only productive, but humane. This is something the best business leaders seem to know almost intuitively but at times is most eloquently expressed by statesmen and philosophers.

Churchill observed, "We make our buildings, then our buildings make us." A building's work is not completed when it is erected, nor an organization chart's when issued. They both must be lived in; the way they are structured can have a considerable impact on the quality of life and work possible in each. Excessive structure is uneconomical and confining. Structure creates walls, internal borders. The self-protective behaviors engendered, and the armies of staff police needed to guard them, all slow a company, dilute its focus, and add unnecessary rigidity.

Unfortunately, more is required to release the behaviors businesses need to succeed than simply demolishing every wall in sight. Some walls *do* bear necessary loads, some demarcate separations that should not blur, and some provide protection from hostile elements. The remedy for bureaucracy is not anarchy and chaos. These merely serve as the breeding ground for the next demagogic leader. Remember what Erich Fromm wrote at the outset of the Second World War: "True freedom is not the absence of structure—letting the employees go off and do whatever they want—but rather a clear structure that enables people to work within established boundaries in an autonomous and creative way." These are boundaries that are not too close, but not too far away.

This book has outlined some of these structures, ones that can serve as positive jumping-off points, not imprisoning barriers. It also urges that wall demolition be accompanied by bridge building. Barrier removal creates vacuums. Mechanisms for connection making do not rise unaided from the rubble. Reinforced jobs, horizontal organizations, dual hierarchies, jobs-as-assignments all require skillful design. Think about the rapidly changing situation in Europe. While the falling of the Berlin Wall may symbolize the end of the old Europe, it will be new linkages, even those that extend underwater like the English Channel tunnel, that will herald Europe's new beginning.

The dome is a much better architectural analogy for corporate structures than the pyramid is. It is strong, economical, and adaptable.

The Hagia Sophia in Istanbul, built fourteen centuries ago, has over its lifetime served as a monument to a victorious emperor, the largest Christian church ever built, a Moslem mosque, and an art museum.

Photo courtesy of the Turkish Government Tourism and Information Office.

Notes

Prologue: Lower Walls

Page

3   "Design a product": "Japan's Smart Secret Weapon," *Business Week*, Aug. 12, 1991, p. 74.

4   André Maginot: James Giblin, *Walls: Defenses Throughout History* (Boston: Little, Brown, 1984).

5   "There's something about": Thomas Stewart, "Brainpower," *Fortune*, June 3, 1991, p. 60. *Fortune*, © 1991 Time Inc. All rights reserved.

5   "The old models": Stan Davis and Bill Davidson, *2020 Vision* (New York: Simon & Schuster, 1991), p. 143.

6   Many of these: Donald Schön, *Beyond the Stable State* (New York: Norton, 1973), pp. 31–60.

6   *Any tendency toward:* Ibid., p. 33.

8   "It is always amazing": Peter Drucker, "FYI," *INC.*, Apr. 1991, p. 14.

Chapter 1: Create a New Breed of Corporation

Page

11   Historically leaders were: Ray Stata, "Organizational Learning— The Key to Management Innovation," *Sloan Management Review*, Spring 1989, pp. 63–64.

12   "Gigantic pieces of": Charles Handy, *The Age of Unreason* (Boston: Harvard Business School Press, 1990), p. 89.

14   Ancient Egyptian buildings: Paul Jacques Grillo, *Form, Function & Design* (New York: Dover, 1960), pp. 55–60.

Page

14   In the twelfth century: Stephen Gardiner, *Inside Architecture* (Englewood Cliffs, N.J.: Prentice-Hall, 1983), pp. 53–55.

16   The word "bureaucracy": Elliott Jaques, "In Praise of Hierarchy," *Harvard Business Review*, Jan.–Feb. 1990, p. 127.

16   "Structure kills": Tom Peters, *Thriving on Chaos* (New York: Knopf, 1987), p. 354.

17   Procter & Gamble: Jolie Solomon and Carol Hymowitz, "P&G Makes Changes," *Wall Street Journal*, Aug. 11, 1987, p. 12.

17   General Motors: Alex Taylor III, "Can GM Remodel Itself?" *Fortune*, Jan. 13, 1992, p. 32.

18   Paul Jacques Grillo: Grillo, op. cit., pp. 129–132, 209.

19   Peter Drucker's vision: Peter Drucker, "The Coming of the New Organization," *Harvard Business Review*, Jan.–Feb. 1988, p. 45.

19   Charles Handy's creative conceptualization: Charles Handy, *The Age of Unreason* (Boston: Harvard Business Review Press, 1990), pp. 87–116.

20   D. Quinn Mills: D. Quinn Mills, *Rebirth of the Corporation* (New York: Wiley, 1991).

20   "A flat web": Neal Boudette, "Networks to Dismantle Old Structures," *Industry Week*, Jan. 16, 1989, p. 29.

Chapter 2: Start With the Work

Page

23   More than half: "A Work-Out for Corporate America," *Economist*, Jan. 7, 1989, p. 55.

23   A group of University: Kim Cameron et al., "Best Practices in White-Collar Downsizing, *Executive*, Aug. 1991, pp. 57–58.

23   A wide-ranging study: Amanda Bennett, "Downsizing Doesn't Necessarily Bring an Upswing in Corporate Profitability," *Wall Street Journal*, June 6, 1991, p. B1.

24   "Expect an organization": David Heenan, "The Downside of Downsizing," *Across the Board*, May 1990, p. 18.

24   Exxon: Peter Nulty, "Exxon's Problem: Not What You Think," *Fortune*, April 23, 1990, p. 204.

Page

24 The *New York Times* charged: Claudia Deutsch, "The Giant With a Black Eye," *New York Times*, Apr. 2, 1989, p. F1.

24 "Accident prone": Chris Welles, "Exxon's Future: What Has Larry Rawl Wrought?" *Business Week*, April 2, 1990, pp. 75–76.

25 "Early retirements have": Harry Levinson, "Trends in Consulting Practice," *Academy of Management Managerial Consultation Division Newsletter*, Nov.–Dec. 1987, p. 2.

25 A survey of *Industry Week*'s: Anne Fisher, "The Downside of Downsizing," *Fortune*, May 23, 1988, p. 42.

25 "I'm obsolete": John Byrne, "Caught in the Middle," *Business Week*, Sept. 12, 1988, p. 88.

25 "There's very little": Thomas Murray, "Bitter Survivors," *Business Month*, May 1987, p. 30.

25 "The cynicism out there": Byrne, op. cit., p. 80.

25 A manager in a major: Ibid., pp. 81–82.

26 The bank's personnel director: "Readers Report," *Business Week*, Oct. 10, 1988, pp. 12–16.

26 "It's tough for them": David Greising, "Continental Bank: Still Jockeying for Position," *Business Week*, Sept. 30, 1991, p. 112.

26 One consultant who studied: Bennett, op. cit., p. B8.

26 The bloat had returned: Ibid.

27 "Large size breeds": John Byrne, "Is Your Company Too Big?" *Business Week*, Mar. 27, 1989, pp. 87–88.

27 "A penalty of size": Ibid., p. 88.

28 One postmortem analysis: Bennett, op. cit., p. B8.

28 The Roman emperor: "Will the Two-Tier Wage System Decline and Fall?" *Business Week*, June 29, 1987.

28 One American company: Gary Hamel and C. K. Prahalad, "Strategic Intent," *Harvard Business Review*, May–June 1989, p. 68.

29 Downsizing is a trap: Ford Worthy, "Japan's Smart Secret Weapon," *Fortune*, Aug. 12, 1991, pp. 73–74.

30 James Bryant: Bennett, op. cit., p. B8.

30 Minnesota Mining and Manufacturing: Kevin Kelly, "3M Run Scared? Forget About It," *Business Week*, Sept. 16, 1991, pp. 59–62.

Page

30   A recent review: Bennett, op. cit., p. B1.

31   Picasso: Davis and Davidson, op. cit., p. 111.

31   Joseph Schumpeter: Ibid., p. 115.

Chapter 3: Look From the Top Down

Page

36   In the late 1980s: Charles Handy, *The Age of Unreason* (Boston: Harvard Business School Press, 1990), p. 122.

37   Michael Porter: Michael Porter, *Competitive Advantage* (New York: Free Press, 1985), pp. 33–61.

38   Philip Selznik: Philip Selznik, *Leadership in Administration* (New York: Harper & Row, 1957), pp. 42–55.

38   More recently they: C. K. Prahalad and Gary Hamel, "The Core Competence of the Corporation," *Harvard Business Review*, May–June 1990, pp. 79–91.

38   "It is not very comforting": Gary Hamel and C. K. Prahalad, "Stategic Intent," *Harvard Business Review*, May–June 1989, p. 71.

38   "Toxic side effects": Ibid., p. 72.

39   Motorola: Gary Hamel and C. K. Prahalad, "Corporate Imagination and Expeditionary Marketing," *Harvard Business Review*, July–Aug. 1991, p. 83.

39   Rubbermaid: Brian Dumaine, "Closing the Innovation Gap," *Fortune*, Dec. 2, 1991, p. 59.

40   Kao: Ikujiro Nonaka, "The Knowledge-Creating Company," *Harvard Business Review*, Nov.–Dec. 1991, p. 103.

40   Ajinomoto: Gary Hamel and C. K. Prahalad, "Corporate Imagination and Expeditionary Marketing," *Harvard Business Review*, July–Aug. 1991, p. 83.

41   "An organization's capacity": Gary Hamel and C. K. Prahalad, "Strategic Intent," *Harvard Business Review*, May–June 1989, p. 68.

42   Alan Kay: Davis and Davidson, op. cit., p. 40.

43   Naval Aviation Depot Corporation: Discussion with the Norfolk Depot's senior management group at meeting on Sept. 26, 1991, at Virginia Beach, Virginia.

Page

44   Two business school professors: Davis and Davidson, op. cit.,
          pp. 81–110.

46   Group called the *mittelstand*: "Think Small," *Business Week*, Nov.
          4, 1991, pp. 58–65.

46   One study, conducted: Hermann Simon, "Secrets of Mid-Sized
          Market Leaders," *World Link*, Nov. 6, 1991, pp. 46–47.

47   "We've picked and chosen": John Byrne, "Is Your Company Too
          Big?" *Business Week*, Mar. 27, 1989, p. 88.

47   Campbell Soup: Bill Saporito, "Campbell Soup Gets Piping
          Hot," *Fortune*, Sept. 9, 1991, pp. 142–148.

47   Kodak: Seth Lubove, "Aim, Focus and Shoot," *Forbes*, Nov. 26,
          1990, pp. 67–70; Joan Rigdon, "Kodak Shuffles Executives . . ."
          Wall Street Journal, Aug. 13, 1991, p. A4.

49   Siemens: Charles Ferguson, "Computers and the Coming of the
          U.S. Keiretsu," *Harvard Business Review*, July–Aug. 1990, p. 61.

Chapter 4: Look From the Bottom Up

Page

50   Peter Drucker: Joseph Badaracco, Jr., *The Knowledge Link* (Boston:
          Harvard Business School Press, 1991), p. 129.

51   "I had always thought:" Erik Calonius, "Smart Moves by Qual-
          ity Champs," *Fortune*, 1991/The New American Century Issue,
          p. 26. *Fortune*, © 1991 Time Inc. All rights reserved.

52   "One way to get": Walter Kiechel III, "Corporate Strategy for the
          1990s," *Fortune*, Feb. 29, 1988, p. 38. *Fortune*, © 1988 Time Inc.
          All rights reserved.

52   "Quite honestly, I": John Byrne, "Caught in the Middle," *Busi-
          ness Week*, Sept. 12, 1988, pp. 83–84.

54   Called "workout,": Mark Potts, "Seeking a Better Idea," *Wash-
          ington Post*, Oct. 7, 1990, p. H1.; Thomas A. Stewart, "GE Keeps
          Those Ideas Coming," *Fortune*, Aug. 12, 1991, pp. 41–49.

54   "Thousands of bad habits": Noel Tichy and Ram Charan,
          "Speed, Simplicity and Self-Confidence," *Harvard Business Re-
          view*, Sept.–Oct. 1989, p. 118.

55   "We've tried to eliminate": Christine Winter and Laurie Cohen,

Page

"A No-Nonsense Leader Brings Continental Bank Back From the Brink," *Washington Post*, Aug. 21, 1988, p. H6.

55   Fewer moving parts: Ibid.

55   "The company junked": "Cost Cutting: How to Do It Right," *Fortune*, Apr. 9, 1990, p. 43. *Fortune*, © 1990 Time Inc. All rights reserved.

55   "For a large organization": Tichy and Charan, op. cit., p. 114.

56   In the late 1980s: George Stalk and Thomas Hout, *Competing Against Time* (New York: Free Press, 1990).

56   Coleman: Brian Dumaine, "Earning More by Moving Faster," *Fortune*, Oct. 7, 1991, pp. 89–91.

57   Geers: "Think Small," *Business Week*, Nov. 4, 1991, p. 60.

57   "They think about time": Kiechel, op. cit., p. 42. *Fortune*, © 1988 Time Inc. All rights reserved.

57   "Quality and cycle time": "Questing for the Best," *Business Week*, Quality 1991 (annual), p. 11.

57   Toyota: George Salk, "Time—The Next Source of Competitive Advantage," *Harvard Business Review*, July–Aug. 1988, p. 48.

59   Perot Systems: speech by Ross Perot on Apr. 29, 1991, Planning Forum annual meeting, Toronto.

59   "As companies grow": Joseph Bower and Thomas Hout, "Fast-Cycle Capability for Competitive Power," *Harvard Business Review*, Nov.–Dec. 1988, p. 111.

59   "Reengineering": Michael Hammer, "Reengineering Work: Don't Automate, Obliterate," *Harvard Business Review*, July–Aug. 1990, pp. 104–112.

61   Heinz: Ronald Henkoff, "Cost Cutting: How to Do It Right," *Fortune*, Apr. 9, 1990, p. 46.

61   Citicorp: Marc Levinson, "Honey, I Shrunk the Bank," *Newsweek*, Feb. 3, 1992, p. 38.

62   Cholesterol and Overhead: Harold McGee, *On Food and Cooking* (New York: Collier Books, 1984), pp. 531–532; Harold Karpman, *Preventing Silent Heart Disease* (New York: Crown, 1989), pp. 47–49; Catherine Macek, "Jack Sprat Was on the Right Track," *Piedmont Airlines*, Feb. 1988, pp. 41–43.

63   LTV: Michael Schroeder, "This 'Barracuda' Is Still on the Attack," *Business Week*, Jan. 20, 1992, pp. 96–97.

Page

63   "No one ever said": Ibid., p. 97.

63   Shell: Peter Schwartz, *The Art of the Long View* (New York: Doubleday, 1991), pp. 3–63.

64   Thomas Hout: Mark Blaxill and Thomas Hout, "The Fallacy of the Overhead Quick Fix," *Harvard Business Review*, July–Aug. 1991, pp. 96–98.

Chapter 5: Repeal the Industrial Revolution

Page

70   "The man whose whole life": As quoted in W. J. Heisler and John Houck, *A Matter of Dignity* (Notre Dame, Ind.: University of Notre Dame Press, 1977), p. 51.

71   The attempt at Volvo: Steven Prokesch, "Edges Fray on Volvo's Brave New Humanistic World," *New York Times*, July 7, 1991, p. F5.

72   This method of: Arthur Stinchcombe, *Information and Organizations* (Berkeley: University of California Press, 1990), p. 44.

72   Each journeyman had: Ibid., p. 40.

73   Small cottage industries: Fernand Braudel, *The Wheels of Commerce, Volume II* (New York: Harper & Row, 1982), pp. 298–300.

73   "From workers the right": Stinchcombe, op. cit., p. 57.

74   "One has the feeling": Henry Mintzberg, *The Structuring of Organizations* (Englewood Cliffs, N.J.: Prentice-Hall, 1979), p. 73.

74   He called this practice: Ibid., p. 74.

74   "The common view": Amy Borrus, "The Navy Tries to Get Its Ship in Shape," *Business Week*, Quality 1991 (annual), p. 134.

75   This keeps Claas: Hermann Simon, "Lessons From Germany's Midsize Giants," *Harvard Business Review*, Mar.–Apr. 1992, pp. 120–121.

75   Recently two maintenance workers: Brian Dumaine, "Unleash Workers and Cut Costs," *Fortune*, May 18, 1992, p. 88.

76   Make sales calls: Terence Pare, "The Big Threat to Big Steel's Future," *Fortune*, July 15, 1991, p. 107.

77   Good construction materials: Mario Salvadori, *Why Buildings Stand Up* (New York: Norton, 1990), pp. 61–62.

Chapter 6: Make Work Whole Again

Page

82   "People who had never": General Electric 1990 Annual Report.

82   Kodak has moved: Henkoff, op. cit., p. 48.

82   IBM has created: Ronald Henkoff, "Make Your Office More Pro-
      ductive," *Fortune*, Feb. 25, 1991, p. 84.

82   Arthur D. Little study: Ranganath Nayak, "Productivity and the
      White Collar," *New York Times*, July 7, 1991.

82   Study conducted by: Henkoff, "Make Your Office More Produc-
      tive," op. cit., p. 73.

83   Saab built: Edgar Schein, "Corporate Teams and Totems," *Across
      the Board*, May 1989, p. 14.

83   Coca-Cola Company surveyed: Robert Tomasko, *Strengthening
      Your Relationships With Store Employees* (Atlanta: Coca-Cola Retail-
      ing Research Council, 1991), p. 41.

84   RailTex: "RailTex," *Forbes*, Oct. 15, 1990, p. 172.

85   Eliminating the warranty costs: Joseph Badaracco, Jr., *The Knowl-
      edge Link* (Boston: Harvard Business School Press, 1991), p. 123.

85   Vanguard Group: "Vanguard Calls 'All Hands on Deck,' " *In the
      Vanguard*, Spring 1992, p. 1.

86   Union Carbide: James Norman, "A New Union Carbide Is
      Slowly Starting to Gel," *Business Week*, Apr. 18, 1988, p. 68.

86   AT&T: Thomas Taylor et al., "Operating Without Supervisors:
      An Experiment," *Organizational Dynamics*, Winter 1987, pp. 26–
      38.

87   Deere & Company: Myron Magnet, "The Resurrection of the
      Rust Belt," *Fortune*, Aug. 15, 1988, pp. 44–45.

89   Texas Instruments: Brian Dumaine, "Who Needs a Boss?" *For-
      tune*, May 7, 1990, pp. 55–58.

89   The Viper: Andrea Rothman, "The Racy Viper Is Already Win-
      ner for Chrysler," *Business Week*, Nov. 4, 1991, pp. 36–38.

89   Ford: James Treece, "How Ford and Mazda Shared the Driver's
      Seat," *Business Week*, Mar. 26, 1990, pp. 94–95.

90   Saved Chrysler $500 million: David Woodruff, "Chrysler May
      Actually Be Turning the Corner," *Business Week*, Feb. 10, 1992,
      p. 32.

Page

91   Japanese management tends: M. Y. Yoshino, *Japan's Managerial System* (Cambridge, Mass.: MIT Press, 1971), pp. 201–203.

93   Levi Strauss: "The Workers of the Future," *Fortune*, 1991 Special Issue: *The New American Century*, pp. 71–72.

93   Corning, Inc.: John Hoerr, "Sharpening Minds for a Competitive Edge," *Business Week*, Dec. 17, 1990, pp. 72–78.

93   Japan Air Lines: "Technology," *Fortune*, May 22, 1989, p. 88.

94   Teli: *Productivity and Employment: Challenges for the 1990s* (Washington, D.C.: U.S. Department of Labor, 1989), pp. 10–11.

94   Monsanto: Laurie Kretchmer, "On the Rise," *Fortune*, Sept. 9, 1991, p. 186.

95   General Mills: Louis Richman, "America's Tough New Job Market," *Fortune*, Feb. 24, 1992, p. 53.

95   Aetna: Brian Dumaine, "Who Needs a Boss?" p. 53.

96   Channel the loads: Mario Salvadori, op. cit., p. 59.

97   Nonmanagerial work: Fred Adair, "It's Time We Made Management a Full-Time Job," *Industry*, Mar. 1987.

97   R. Roosevelt Thomas: R. Roosevelt Thomas, Jr., "From Affirmative Action to Affirming Diversity," *Harvard Business Review*, Mar.–Apr. 1990, p. 116; R. Roosevelt Thomas, Jr., *Beyond Race and Gender* (New York: AMACOM, 1991), pp. 46–47.

97   Live under the same conditions: Mao Tse-tung, *On Guerrilla Warfare* (New York: Praeger, 1961), pp. 91–92.

97   Sam Walton: Sam Walton, "Sam Walton in His Own Words," *Fortune*, June 29, 1992, p. 106.

98   Saturn: Dorothy Williams, "A Different Kind of Car," *Case Alumnus*, Summer 1991, p. 3.

98   Mars, Inc.: Joel Brenner, "Planet of the M&M's," *Washington Post Magazine*, Apr. 12, 1992, pp. 13–19.

Chapter 7: Structure Horizontally

Page

101   Structures bear loads: Mario Salvadori, op. cit., pp. 43–89.

102   Container of space: William Caudill, William Pena, and Paul

Page

Kennon, *Architecture and You* (New York: Watson-Guptill, 1981), p. 15.

102   Dynamic space: Ibid., p. 52.

103   Several contemporary American architects: Ibid., pp. 21–33.

103   "Their bones show": Ibid., p. 25.

104   Some philosophers look: Ibid., p. 171.

106   Louis Sullivan: Bill Risebero, *Modern Architecture and Design* (Cambridge, Mass.: MIT Press, 1983), pp. 128–133.

107   Many Japanese companies: D. Eleanor Westney, "Knowledge Creation: Japan vs. the West," *Harvard Business Review*, Jan.–Feb. 1992, pp. 156–157.

107   Clout of a giant: Brian Dumaine, "Is Big Still Good?" *Fortune*, Apr. 20, 1992, pp. 50–51.

107   Bill Gates: Ibid., pp. 56–60.

108   *Of* the hill: Malise Ruthven, "Architecture: Frank Lloyd Wright— An Exclusive Look at the Palmer House in Ann Arbor, Michigan," *Architectural Digest*, Mar. 1992, p. 42.

108   These pagodas have: Louis Hellman, *Architecture for Beginners* (New York: Writers & Readers, 1988), p. 70.

110   Short paths are: Grillo, op. cit., pp. 208–209.

Chapter 8: Organize Around Customers and Processes

Page

111   "We became much more aggressive": Claudia Deutsch, "The Efficiencies of Going Public," *New York Times*, Sept. 22, 1991, p. F25.

111   John Langford: Jack Willoughby, "Buried Treasure," *Forbes*, May 18, 1987.

112   Oryx Energy Company: Peter Nulty, "Oil's Prospects: A Better Decade," *Fortune*, Apr. 22, 1991, p. 146.

112   "I would rather see": Brian Dumaine, "What the Leaders of Tomorrow See," *Fortune*, July 3, 1989, p. 58. *Fortune*, © 1989 Time Inc. All rights reserved.

112   "Spends more time": Ibid. *Fortune*, © 1989 Time Inc. All rights reserved.

Page

112 *Joint ventures:* Louis Kraar, "Your Rivals Can Be Your Allies," *Fortune*, Mar. 27, 1989, pp. 66–72.

113 Wal-Mart: Bruce Caldwell, "Wal-Mart to Middlemen: Bye, Bye, Thanks to EDI," *Information Week*, Dec. 9, 1991, p. 11.

113 Visa: "Dee Ward Hock," *Fortune*, Mar. 11, 1991, p. 101.

114 "Managers from companies": Benn Konsynski and F. Warren McFarlan, "Information Partnerships—Shared Data, Shared Scale," *Harvard Business Review*, Sept.–Oct. 1990, p. 114.

114 Audrey Freedman: "Why Smokestack America Doesn't Quake at the Word 'Recession,' " *Business Week*, Sept. 11, 1989, p. 101.

114 This unicellular microscopic animal: William T. Keeton, *Biological Science* (New York: Norton, 1967), p. 178.

114 Illinois Tool Works: Ronald Henkoff, "The Ultimate Nuts & Bolts Co.," *Fortune*, July 16, 1990, pp. 70–73.

115 Siemens: Brian Dumaine, "Is Big Still Good?" *Fortune*, Apr. 20, 1992, p. 56.

115 Swissair: D. Quinn Mills, op. cit., p. 133.

115 Sears, Roebuck & Company: Kevin Kelly, "At Sears, the More Things Change . . ." *Business Week*, Nov. 12, 1990, p. 66.

115 Some formats, such as: Susan Caminiti, "Sears Need: More Speed," *Fortune*, July 15, 1991, p. 90.

116 Hewlett-Packard: Robert Hof, "Suddenly, Hewlett-Packard Is Doing Everything Right," *Business Week*, Mar. 23, 1992, p. 88.

116 Niagara Mowhawk Power: Stephanie Losee, "Revolution From Within," *Fortune*, June 1, 1992, p. 112.

116 "So much an assembly line": Henkoff, op. cit., p. 72.

116 USAA: Thomas Teal, "Service Comes First," *Harvard Business Review*, Sept.–Oct. 1991, p. 119.

117 Merck: Joseph Weber, "Merck Needs More Gold From the White Coats," *Business Week*, Mar. 18, 1991, pp. 103–104.

118 Paul Allaire: Thomas Stewart, "The Search for the Organization of Tomorrow," *Fortune*, May 18, 1992, p. 97.

119 Lawrence Bossidy: Ibid., p. 96.

122 *Fortune:* Thomas Moore, "Goodbye, Corporate Staff," *Fortune*, Dec. 21, 1987, p. 65.

Chapter 9: Make Each Level Count

Page

127 Whose singular talent: Paul Carroll, "Computer Data Indicate," *Wall Street Journal*, Aug. 7, 1991, p. A4.

127 Two Harvard Business School professors: Robert Hayes and Ramchandran Jaikumar, "Manufacturing's Crisis," *Harvard Business Review*, Sept.–Oct. 1988, pp. 77–85.

128 Right Associates: "Career Expectations and Attitudes of Today's College Students," *The Right Research Report No. 3*, 1990.

128 Robert Levering: Robert Levering, *A Great Place to Work* (New York: Random House, 1988), pp. 169–170.

128 Even worse psychology: Edgar Schein, "Corporate Teams and Totems," *Across the Board*, May 1989, pp. 12–14.

128 Larry Hirschhorn: Larry Hirschhorn and Thomas Gilmore, "The New Boundaries of the 'Boundaryless' Company," *Harvard Business Review*, May–June 1992, p. 110.

129 People Express: Levering, op. cit., p. 169.

129 Irrational behavior: Abraham Zaleznik, *The Managerial Mystique* (New York: Harper & Row, 1989), p. 37.

129 "An idea in search of": Andrall Pearson, "Corporate Redemption and the Seven Deadly Sins," *Harvard Business Review*, May–June 1992, p. 71.

131 Elliott Jaques: Jaques, op. cit., p. 131.

132 Asea Brown Boveri, Ltd.: "The Euro-Gospel According to Percy Barnevik," *Business Week*, July 23, 1990, p. 65.

132 Only 50 employees: William Taylor, "The Logic of Global Business," *Harvard Business Review*, Mar.–Apr. 1991, p. 99.

133 Changes of state: Jaques, op. cit., p. 130.

134 Jaques's most important observation: Elliott Jaques and Stephen Clement, *Executive Leadership* (Arlington, Va.: Cason Hall, 1991), p. 111.

Chapter 10: Fuse Knowledge to Power

Page

139 Two professors: Gene Dalton and Paul Thompson, *Novations: Strategies for Career Management* (Glenview, Ill.: Scott, Foresman, 1986).

Page

139   Each stage differs: Gene Dalton, Paul Thompson, and Raymond
          Price, "The Four Stages of Professional Careers," *Organizational
          Dynamics*, Summer 1977, p. 22.

143   They take strong positions: Dalton and Thompson, op. cit., pp.
          159–177.

144   Map of the future: Ibid., pp. 137–140.

144   "Must learn to think": Dalton, Thompson, and Price, op. cit., p.
          35.

145   And is associated with: Guy Benveniste, *Professionalizing the Or-
          ganization* (San Francisco: Jossey-Bass, 1987), pp. 28–55.

145   "Tend to fragment": Zaleznik, op. cit., p. 115.

145   Standing in their field: Joseph Raelin, *The Clash of Cultures* (Bos-
          ton: Harvard Business School Press, 1985), pp. 2–3.

146   Microsoft: Brenton Schlender, "How Bill Gates Keeps the Magic
          Going," *Fortune*, June 18, 1990, p. 84.

146   Corning Glass Works: Anthony Ramirez, "Making Better Use of
          Older Workers," *Fortune*, Jan. 30, 1989, p. 184.

146   A fast-food operator: Claudia Deutsch, "Holding On to Techni-
          cal Talent," *New York Times*, Nov. 16, 1986, p. 9.

146   Semco S.A.: Ricardo Semler, "Managing Without Managers,"
          Harvard Business Review, Sept.–Oct. 1989, p. 78.

Chapter 11: Provide Two Paths to the Top

Page

148   Braun: Stewart Toy, "His Spartan Look Is the Essence of Braun,"
          Business Week, Innovation 1990, p. 178.

149   Fresh solutions: Simon Ramo, *Cure for Chaos* (New York: McKay,
          1969).

149   Microsoft: Brenton Schlender, op. cit., p. 84.

150   Lawrence Bossidy: Thomas Stewart, "The Search for the Orga-
          nization of Tomorrow," *Fortune*, May 18, 1992, p. 96

151   Hospitals could not serve: Benveniste, op. cit., pp. 90–91.

151   Time, Inc.: Bill Saporito, "The Inside Story of Time Warner,"
          Fortune, Nov. 20, 1989, p. 174.

Page

152   *Nemawashi:* Keitaro Hasegawa, *Japanese-Style Management* (Tokyo: Kodansha International, 1986), pp. 51–53.

152   Arthur Fry: Claudia Deutsch, "Holding On to Technical Talent," *New York Times*, Nov. 16, 1986, p. 9.

152   Columbia University study: Ibid.

153   Two long chains: David Sylvester and Lynn Klotz, *The Gene Age* (New York: Scribner, 1983), p. 154.

154   Veneers such as glass: Grillo, op. cit., p. 73.

155   "Work very hard": Gary Hamel and C. K. Prahalad, "Corporate Imagination and Expeditionary Marketing," *Harvard Business Review*, July–Aug. 1991, p. 83.

157   Alfred Sloan: Zaleznik, op. cit., pp. 28–29.

158   More and more: Raelin, op. cit., p. 101.

158   "Merely machines": Tom Peters, "Tomorrow's Companies," *Economist*, Mar. 4, 1989, p. 21.

159   Toyota: Alex Taylor III, "Why Toyota Keeps Getting Better and Better and Better," *Fortune*, Nov. 19, 1990, p. 72.

160   NutraSweet: Brian O'Reilly, "Is Your Company Asking Too Much?" *Fortune*, Mar. 12, 1990, p. 41.

160   "Envelope supervision": Benveniste, op. cit., p. 72.

160   "Servant leadership": Robert Greenleaf, *Servant Leadership* (New York: Paulist Press, 1977).

160   Robert Taylor: Walter Kiechel III, "The Leader as Servant," *Fortune*, May 4, 1992, p. 122.

161   The more typical perversion: Walter Kiechel III, "When Management Regresses," *Fortune*, Mar. 9, 1992, p. 158.

161   "Sorry, you seem to": Josh Weston, "Sustaining Long-Term Growth," *Executive Summary: 1991 Planning Forum International Conference*, p. 39.

161   "If anything goes bad": Pat Riley, *Showtime* (New York: Warner Books, 1988), p. 133.

162   Siemens: Brian Dumaine, "Is Big Still Good?" *Fortune*, Apr. 20, 1992, p. 56.

Chapter 12: Question All the Answers

Page

164 Amsterdam's ING Bank building: *Building With a Difference: ING Bank Head Office* (Amsterdam: Internationale Nederlanden Bank, 1992).

166 Kyocera: Gene Bylinsky, "The Hottest High-Tech Company in Japan," *Fortune*, Jan. 1, 1990, pp. 83–88.

167 Cypress Semiconductors: T. J. Rogers, "No Excuses Management," *Harvard Business Review*, July–Aug. 1990, pp. 87–89.

168 Chaparral Steel: Tom Peters, "Management's Greatest Crime— Ignoring Worker's Talent," *Washington Business Journal*, Oct. 5, 1987, p. 7.

169 "Nontraditional" plant closings: James Treece, "Doing It Right, Till the Last Whistle," *Business Week*, Apr. 6, 1992, pp. 58–59.

169 Recycled retirees: David Kirkpatrick, "Smart New Ways to Use Temps," *Fortune*, Feb. 15, 1988, p. 116.

171 Improvement in white-collar productivity: Thane Peterson, "Can Corporate America Get Out From Under Its Overhead?" *Business Week*, May 18, 1992, p. 102.

172 "The GPO, established": "Reports and Testimony: October 1990," U.S. General Accounting Office, Washington, D.C.

172 Libby-Owens-Ford: Peter Krass, "Outsourcing Twice Removed," *Information Week*, Nov. 4, 1991, p. 25.

173 ABB: Carla Rapoport, "A Tough Swede Invades the U.S.," *Fortune*, June 29, 1992, p. 77.

173 Pirelli: "The 10 Key Functions Today's Planners Perform," *Business International Special Report*, Aug. 1991, p. 2.

173 IBM: David Kirkpatrick, "Breaking Up IBM," *Fortune*, July 27, 1992, pp. 53–54.

173 Toro: Brian Dumaine, "Closing the Innovation Gap," *Fortune*, Dec. 2, 1991, p. 59.

174 Michael Porter's research: Michael Porter, "The Competitive Advantage of Nations," *Harvard Business Review*, Mar.–Apr. 1990, p. 92.

174 Reengineering advocates: John Byrne, "Management's New Gurus," *Business Week*, Aug. 21, 1992, p. 50.

Page

174   City of Phoenix: David Osborne and Ted Gaebler, *Reinventing Government* (Reading, Mass.: Addison-Wesley, 1992), pp. 76–78.

177   Visualizing three-dimensional buildings: Howard Rheingold, *Virtual Reality* (New York: Simon & Schuster, 1991), p. 42.

178   *Virtual reality:* Ibid., pp. 13–46.

Epilogue: Build Domes, Not Pyramids

Page

180   Domes are structural configurations: Mario Salvadori, *Why Buildings Stand Up*, pp. 225–230.

181   At times top leaders: John Huey, "Secrets of Great Second Bananas," *Fortune*, May 6, 1991, pp. 64–76.

183   Architecture is not: Witold Rybczynski, *The Most Beautiful House in the World* (New York: Viking Penguin, 1989), p. 3.

183   Gastronomy and cooking: Ibid., p. 50.

183   A long bridge: Thomas Teal, "Service Comes First," *Harvard Business Review*, Sept.–Oct. 1991.

184   "We make our": J. Mordaunt Crook, "We Are Where We Live," *New York Times Book Review*, Jan. 5, 1992, p. 21.

184   "True freedom is": Erich Fromm, *Escape From Freedom* (New York: Rinehart, 1941).

Index